Marie-Claude Foster

Management Skills for Project Leaders
What to do when you do not know what to do

Birkhäuser

658.404
F75m

Author:
Marie-Claude Foster
Centre for International Child Health
Institute of Child Health
University College London
30 Guilford Street
London WC1N 1 EH
England

A CIP catalogue record for this book is available from the
Library of Congress, Washington D.C., USA

Deutsche Bibliothek Cataloging-in-Publication Data
Management skills for project leaders : what to do when you do not know what
to do / Marie-Claude Foster. - Basel ; Boston ; Berlin : Birkhäuser, 2001
  ISBN 3-7643-6423-8

ISBN 3-7643-6423-8 Birkhäuser Verlag, Basel – Boston – Berlin

© 2001 Birkhäuser Verlag, P.O. Box 133, CH-4010 Basel, Switzerland
Birkhäuser is a member of the BertelsmannSpringer Publishing Group
Cover design: Micha Lotrovsky, CH-4106 Therwil, Switzerland
Printed on acid-free paper produced from chlorine-free pulp. TCF ∞
Printed in Germany
ISBN 3-7643-6423-8
9 8 7 6 5 4 3 2 1   www.birkhauser.ch

To my parents

Table of contents

Preface

This book is aimed at managers and project leaders working in a variety of settings in low- and middle-income countries. The main purpose of this book is to bring to people working in the field the up-to-date thoughts on and approaches to management. Recent thinking and theories such as complexity theory, quantum thinking and postmodernism have radical implications for the way we view organisations and the practice of management. Many of the models of management still offered to project leaders and managers are obsolete and not very useful in the light of a chaotic and turbulent world. We need other models to guide us and very different skills from those advocated by the old paradigm. An important aspect of this book is to facilitate the development of these skills which managers and project leaders require so as not only to survive, but to flourish and succeed in the chaotic world of work.

The book contains concepts, thoughts and propositions for practising managers and project leaders, but these remain suggestions. The discerning reader will adopt and reject some of the ideas presented here – and this is a good way of using such a book. There are no blueprints for managers. At best, we have guidelines which the individual manager needs to adapt to the situation and the context in which she operates. Many of the ideas presented here do work. This I know from the many accounts of past students who have been exposed to this material. I am particularly grateful to those students who have taken the time to give me long-term feedback. The evidence suggests that the material presented here has facilitated the work of many of the participants in my workshops and courses and that it has been a source of enlightenment and inspiration not only at work but also in their personal lives. My hope is that readers of this small text will also benefit in the same way.

The book relies heavily on the work of two prominent authors in the field of management and organisational dynamics. These are Ralph Stacey and Petruska Clarkson. As the readers will note, their writings feature prominently in the list of further reading. I strongly recommend that interested project leaders and managers consult their books and publications. I have used and adapted many of their ideas to both governmental and non-governmental organisations in low- and mid-dle-income countries. The work presented here, while drawing on these notions, is inevitably my own interpretation of these concepts. I therefore take full responsibility for the contents of the present book.

Another aim of this publication is that of simplifying many of the original concepts to make them available to a wider audience. There is danger in doing so and I am well aware that at times the present book may offer too simplistic a picture. The reader has to be aware that the issues raised are highly complex.

Chapter 1 considers the inadequacies of the old paradigm in man-agement and looks at the implications of complexity theory for the project leader. Chapter 2 looks at negative and positive strategies in the light of complexity and uncertainty while chapter 3 focusses on the process of decision-making. Chapter 4 looks at important skills which are helpful to us in dealing with uncertainty and complexity in work organisations. Chapters 5, 6 and 7 consider the importance of continu-ous learning and development for project leaders, managers, workers and work organisations. The final two chapters address the issue of change in organisations and consider the skills of the change agent. There are mini case studies to illustrate important notions. Although the issues raised pertain to real-life organisations, the case studies themselves are fictitious. More importantly, there are a number of activities in each chapter. Readers are encouraged to carry out the activities as these enable reflection and encourage the application of concepts to real-life situations.

Acknowledgements

We all have our own teachers and mentors in life. One such mentor for me is Petruska Clarkson who has done so much to guide, stimulate, inspire and challenge me in my work. I am, therefore, greatly indebted to her. I should like to thank my partner, John, and my head of department, Andrew Tomkins, who have provided much support and who have read and commented on an earlier version of this book. I also thank Erdmuthe Gravenhorst for editing the final version. Finally, this book would not exist without the constant encouragement, feedback and stimulation of the many participants from all over the world, who have contributed and engaged in a rich dialogue with me during the many workshops and courses which I facilitate. This book is dedicated to all these very special people.

Thank you to Coleman Barks for permission to reproduce Rumi's poems from "One-handed Basket Weaving-Poems on the theme of Work", Versions by Coleman Barks, Maypop, Athens, Georgia.

Chapter 1   Dealing with uncertainty and complexity

The issue

Work organisations operate in conditions of uncertainty and complexity. Most project leaders and managers have been taught models which are only useful when the task is relatively simple and when conditions are relatively certain. To be an effective manager in a turbulent and complex world we need to draw on different models and understand the nature of the chaotic and complex world in which we live and work.

Complexity in the work situation

"In our area we rely on crops to provide us with an income for the project but we are always uncertain… no-one can tell us what the crops will be like. There are loads of things we know about what to do with plants, but no-one can tell you what is going to happen."

"In this project we know where we want to go and that we want to try to help people, but we are never sure of our outcomes."

"At our meetings, we plan what we want to do, this amount of things but there are inevitably some other problems we did not foresee. We are not sure of what is going to happen, however well we have planned."

"You plan and just as you arrive at a certain point, you have to replan again, after seeing how it is going. Part of what we had decided might have gone "to plan" but parts of the original plan may look widely different."

These quotations from project leaders illustrate the uncertain nature of much of project work. Most of the activities undertaken in projects are also very complex. Those who express these opinions come from a variety of fields: health services, both curative and preventive, community development, relief and emergency services, community disability services, water and sanitation. The degree of uncertainty and complexity will vary according to the work we do but at some level all human systems are intrinsically complex systems. A community hospital or an irrigation system will have high levels of certainty and relative simplicity in areas where the task is of a mainly technical nature. Those who provide services in refugee camps or are involved in community development find that their work is amazingly complex and most outcomes are uncertain. Of course, the level of uncertainty and of complexity fluctuates in many situations. Technical tasks are predominantly of the relatively simple/certain category while general managerial duties and any work which involves people are both complex and uncertain.

In recent years, drawing on complexity theory, we have been able to gain a better understanding of the nature of the complex and uncertain world in which managers operate. We also know what skills are useful to managers if they wish to be efficient in an ever-changing turbulent world.

This chapter provides a better understanding of the setting in which we function and the implications of complexity and uncertainty for managers.

Complexity as normal

Natural systems including human systems are complex, non-linear systems. Complex is not the same as complicated. When something is complicated we are able to break it into its simpler parts. In a complex system we are unable to do so. All the parts of a complex system are interrelated, thus its components cannot easily be isolated and the whole cannot be reduced to its parts. Thus when dealing with complex systems we have to take a holistic approach, because the whole in a complex system is much more than the sum of its parts.

In a simple linear system, we can identify the parts and there is a simple cause-and-effect relationship between the parts. In non-linear systems all the parts of the system are interrelated and this connectedness means that it is difficult to isolate simple cause and effect. Our knowledge about complex systems comes from a variety of disciplines: quantum physics, the natural sciences, ecology, mathematics, sociology and psychology. Complexity theory provides us with useful analogies in thinking about work organisations.

Work organisations as complex systems

Human systems, and work organisations as human systems, are non-linear feedback systems subject to both negative and positive feedback. What we do, what we fail to do, our background, our beliefs, our expectations and what we experience are constantly being fed back into the new decisions and the choices we make in the present and about the future. Non-linear feedback systems show certain important characteristics and these features have crucial implications for managing these systems. A major attribute is that the system itself produces uncertainty and complexity. This means that however much we attempt to control the system, we inevitably will encounter much that we cannot control. In complex systems, very small changes and very minute interventions can potentially amplify to such an extent as to lead to totally different outcomes from what was predicted. This is known technically as "sensitive dependence on initial conditions" – popularly known as the "butter-fly-wing-effect" in that the proverbial butterfly flapping its wings somewhere in the world can potentially lead to a disturbance in the atmosphere which amplifies and may lead to a storm somewhere else in the world. In work organisations also, minute changes may intensify and lead to a disturbance in the organised plans of an organisation. We cannot tell in advance which minute changes will amplify, how they will do so and what the consequences will be, especially in the long term. Therefore, uncertainty and complexity are **normal** features for work organisations and projects. The diffi-culties, the turbulence and the chaos which work organisations and projects experience may not be the result of "bad" management but a consequence of the intrinsic nature of human systems. Added to this intrinsic complexity and uncertainty which arise from the sys-tem itself, is the fact that work organisations are not isolated from the external world. Uncertainty and complexity also occur from the interrelatedness between the organisation and the external environment. The policies of governments nationally and internationally, the fluctuations in the economic system, changes in the local communities – all these affect our projects whether we like it or not. But from what we have said earlier, uncertainty and complexity also arise from within the project itself. Very minute changes can also have a profound effect on the whole system. For example, a different style of working, a new member of staff joining us, or new technology being introduced, all these can potentially influence and disrupt the system at a very deep level. Extremely small fluctuations may lead to substantial change in the system; generally it takes some time for these changes to be apparent. While we can foresee some of those, many of the outcomes of what we undertake in projects are unpredictable in advance.

For many projects, the nature of the task itself can be full of uncertainty and complexity. Primary health care or community-based rehabilitation is full of ambiguities, contradictions, complications and intricacies. To summarise, we find that to a large extent, complexities and uncertainties arise from within the system itself and the interrelationship between the organisation and the external environment. Therefore, when managers discover that performance is uneven, this may be due to the fact that the system itself is erratic and changeable and may not be the result of inefficient management. Consequently, managers and project leaders need to be confident and skilled in handling uncertainty and complexity in the work place.

The limitations of traditional linear models

Unfortunately, many of the models which we have been taught are not effective when we have to deal with uncertainty and complexity. We need new models to guide us. As was mentioned in the introduction to this book, traditional models of management are based on logical, rational reasoning which operate well when things are relatively simple and certain. These are mechanical models which serve us well when we are dealing with the known and the simple. But they do not help us when we have to deal with uncertainty and complexity.

Traditional models offered to managers are of the linear type. By this, we mean that there is a belief in a simple cause-and-effect model and that good management consists of identifying the neat steps which lead to a desired outcome. This is a step-by-step model, where the assumption is that we can plan in advance and where implementation consists of carefully following these steps to achieve the result which we want. An underlying supposition of this paradigm is that the well-functioning organisation is a stable one in total equilibrium. When we adopt the linear mentality, a specific intervention has only one specific outcome. We shall go on to see that in work organisations, we are inevitably dealing with multi-causality except for a few simple technical matters. In a later chapter, we shall examine how stability is destructive to work organisations, because those projects which work from this model are simply repeating the past when the world around them has changed. In many low- and middle-income countries many projects are continuously repeating past patterns which are not appropriate for the environment in which they are functioning. Traditional management models also suggest that there are blueprints and prescriptions for management. They propose that we can control organisations and projects. Unfortunately, this is not the case. In a complex and uncertain world, there are no easy clear answers, there are at all times several answers, several possibilities and several choices and we are never totally sure that the path we choose will turn out to be the "correct" one. Management is about taking risks, including taking risks when we are unable to tell what will be the end result of our intervention. It demands taking responsibility for what we do, it demands courage and it also demands humility and the ability to be in a state of continuous learning.

Table 1 summarises some of the major characteristics of complexity as shown in work organisations. We shall now look at these in greater detail.

The future is always uncertain

Although we like to plan and have aspirations for the future, the future is always uncertain. Human beings cannot control the future. At its extremes, this shows itself internationally through the great

Table 1.1. Summary of important notions about complex systems

– The future is always uncertain.

– People organise spontaneously through a self-organising
  process and organisations can self-organise as stable "ossified"
  systems, or in a state of disintegration, or in a transition state
  known as the edge of chaos.

– Self-organisation – when patterns emerge from disorder and
  chaos – is a spontaneous process which is the result of
  "agents" interacting with each other. Human beings interact
  with each other by having conversations, hence relationships
  are crucial for work organisations.

– In complex systems, strategies emerge; they cannot be planned
  in advance and these strategies emerge from the ordinary conversations which people have with each other.

– Paradox is a characteristic of the "edge of chaos".

– The edge of chaos is a potentially highly creative space.

– Control is not possible in complex systems and there are
  important implications for managers and project leaders.

tragedies which create turmoil in societies, e.g., wars, earthquakes,
floods. Less dramatically, societies are constantly in a state of flux
with, for example, changes in the economy and socio-cultural
change and through an increase in formal education. Ecologically,
economically, politically and socially the future is always uncertain.
At the individual level, we also experience the uncertainty of the
future. Although we would like to foresee what will happen, the
future is both unknown and unknowable. We can have aspirations,
we can have dreams and we can have desires, but we cannot be certain of what will happen. Additionally, work organisations do not
operate in isolation from turbulent, unstable and fluctuating envi-
ronments. They are affected by that external environment whether
or not people are conscious of that influence.

Until a few years ago, many health workers had a job for life. In recent years, however, in many countries this pattern has changed or is in the process of changing. Many individuals are completely unprepared for this. They have organised their lives as if they will have a stable, secure job for the whole of their working lives. They have planned as if the future was certain. These people are completely unprepared for situations such as redundancy, early retirement, changing jobs and having to retrain.

Tembe has prepared his five-year plan for the health project he manages in a rural area. The funders insist that he provide them with such a plan. He is asked to provide hard indicators which can easily be measured at the end of each year but, more importantly, they demand that he assure them of what the outcome of this project will be in 5 years. Tembe holds meetings with the community and his workers and produces a very impressive report which the funders appreciate. At the end of the first year, Tembe has to check that he is on target to satisfy the demands of the funders. However, very few of the things which he had predicted have actually happened. He has appointed the staff he requires. But the nurse has strained her back and is unable to work for some time. He can only pay for a part time replacement for her. The auxiliary nurses do not like the new nurse and are sabotaging the project. There has been a local election and the new people now in power do not support the project. Most importantly, there has been a devaluation of the local currency and everything which he has to purchase costs much more that what he had previously envisaged. Tembe feels very depressed and fearful about the future and he does not know what to do to deal with the situation.

Implications of an uncertain future for project leaders

Being able to tolerate the fact that the future is both unknown and unknowable is an important skill for project leaders.

This means that when we begin a project we are inevitably engaged in an innovative journey, one which will reveal itself as we go along. It does not mean that the journey will be totally unknown. It will be guided by our dreams and by our aspirations. Although we have no control over the future, we can influence that future.

   Projects in low- and middle-income countries are inevitably innovative journeys because both the context and the people involved are in a
constant state of flux. Users express the need for a service and then
decide that this is not exactly what they wanted. Politicians determine
the way forward for a nation, and then find out that they cannot finance
what they want to implement. An idea works remarkably well in one
community but fails miserably when transported to a neighbouring
area. Therefore, project work in middle- and low-income countries
truly exists in turbulent times. At the international level, people agree
that the only thing about which we can now be certain is change itself
and that the pace of change for most of us has become indisputably
vertiginous. Project leaders need to be able to step into the unknown
and to face the empty space which is the future. Dealing with the anxiety which we experience as we face this unknown and unknowable
future is an important feature of the work of managers and of project
leaders.

Long-term plans are problematic

Managers and project leaders produce long-term plans; plans for the
next 3 or 5 years are quite common. But these plans regularly
become outdated and have to be reviewed. At the end of the period
it is not unusual to find out that the organisation has actually been
doing something quite different from what was stated in the long-
term plan. Stacey (1992) queries the need to write these long-term
plans if we have to keep changing them as we go along. An uncertain future means that any long-term planning is highly problematic. A plan is a chain of operations and steps which one intends to
undertake in a predetermined given order. Research shows that in
practice managers have to keep changing their predicted plans of
action. If they are regularly altering what they were expecting to
execute, one can argue that what they have prepared is no longer a
plan, as they are not following the sequence of actions which they
proposed at the beginning. Most managers and project leaders
engage in long-term planning and for many this is the sign of the
"good, effective" manager. Many project leaders have been trained
to do so, as traditional linear management models stress the impor-

tance of planning. Funders, executive and governing boards also expect managers to engage in long-term forecasts. Another, often unconscious, reason why we like engaging in these forecasts and drawing plans is that doing so gives us the illusion of being in control of uncertainty. Deep down we may consciously or unconsciously worry about the uncertainty of the future, but if we have our plans and our strategies we feel somehow that we are in control. As Stacey (1992) points out, long-term forecasting often turns out to be a fictional exercise and strategic planning meetings are rituals in which we usually engage as a result of tradition. We have always written out long-term action plans and we have always had meetings to discuss these; so we keep on doing so. Time is spent – some would say wasted – producing these long-term plans which we have to keep changing as the future unfolds.

In the real world, managers and project leaders will be asked to write up their 5- and 10-year plans. Sometimes we do not have the power to refuse to do so. In these cases, we can simply produce an idea of what we think we will achieve and how we are going to go about it, as at the end of the day anyone can write a plan. The astute manager produces her plan because she is asked to do so. However, she is prepared for the unknown and does not manage totally according to this plan, because she knows that many long-term plans will simply not work. There are too many unknown possibilities for us to be totally sure that they will work. We can prepare long-term plans if they keep others happy but we do not manage according to these plans. We acknowledge that the future is unknown to us. This does not mean, however, that we cannot have our aspirations and our dreams. These are important. Dreams and aspirations will influence our future. Project leaders therefore need to engage in a voyage of discovery where the journey makes itself known as we go along but which is guided by our hopes and aspirations. The route we take as we move in the direction of our dreams may be full of surprises and we may alter these dreams as we go along to take into account the changes taking place around us. In a later chapter, we shall look at the skills we need to be able to take decisions and not falter in the face of uncertainty.

Activity 1.1

Consider the long-term plans which you have produced in the past for your project.

- **Was the implementation of the plan problem-free or did you experience difficulties?**
- **Did you keep strictly to the plan?**
- **Were there any changes and if so what were these changes?**

Self-organisation in work organisations: from ossification to disintegration and the edge of chaos

Relating to other people is probably the most important activity which affects our strategies in the workplace. The quality of our relationship is therefore crucial for effective management. People are always self-organising and they do so in their ordinary conversations. Sometimes people relate and organise themselves in fixed patterns either in a very stabilized way – ossification – or in a highly unstable, very turbulent manner – disintegration. These ways of interacting and relating become repetitive and the system organises itself in either a state of ossification or a state of disintegration.

Organisations which do not thrive and are not effective operate in a stage of ossification or disintegration

Organisations, which are not doing well, occupy either of two extremes: a state of ossification or a state of disintegration. Think of ossification and disintegration as being at two ends of a continuum and the chaotic edge being in the middle of this continuum.

Ossification ——— Chaos ——— Disintegration

Ossification refers to organisations which are very stable, fixed and rigid in their practices. The assumption is that they operate mainly in a state of certainty. They believe that there are definite, precise and clear answers. This is a black-or-white world. These organisations are unyielding and inflexible. They presume that work can be neatly organised and planned and that we can control the world in which we live. Rigid procedures, rules and systems are the means by which they attempt to be in control.

Bureaucratic organisations belong to that category. Many government departments in low- and middle-income countries are ossified. The organisation is governed by rules which are to be strictly adhered to. Change is the great anathema for these work settings, which often behave as if the world around them is not changing at all. The organisation works in very much the same way from the day it started and engages in repeating the past. This model may, however, be an appropriate one if the aim of a project or of an organisation is to maintain stability and to ensure continuity with the past. It is also an adequate model for settings which operate in a state of certainty and where the task is simple.

Disintegration, which means to separate into parts, to fragment and to break up refers to organisations which are doing just that and therefore are in a state of instability. As with the ossified organisation, those in a state of disintegration also believe in a black-and-white world where there are clear answers which they are searching for in the midst of their busy-ness. Some NGO projects are in a state of disintegration, with high levels of activity, constant flux and incessant superficial change.

Individuals in these organisations tend to replicate the characteristics of the workplace. In ossified organisations, we may find people who are rigid and inflexible and like the comfort of rules, procedures and set plans, which means that they only have to obey and do not have to think for themselves. When things do not work, which is often the case, as projects usually have to deal with both complexity and uncertainty, people can always find someone to blame or they blame the system. There is then a frantic search for more rigid systems and procedures, the search being for the one right answer. Innovative and creative workers find it stressful to work for such organisations and they often leave.

In organisations which are in a state of disintegration, people talk of "being all over the place". There is a great deal of busy ness, but this activity does not necessarily lead to much in terms of productivity. The hyperactivity often induces very high levels of stress in the organisation. In real life, of course, organisations fluctuate along the continuum described above. We also need to note that complete disintegration, the "death" of an organisation, is not necessarily a bad thing. Projects and organisations sometimes need to end. Occasionally, one meets organisations and projects which should have ended but keep on existing. These are projects which should have "died" but which their leaders are maintaining. They often serve no purpose at all, apart from keeping their members employed.

The edge of chaos – both order and disorder

There is, however, a third space which projects and work organisations can occupy. This third space, which is potentially very creative and from which new patterns, new order and innovation emerge, is known as the "edge of chaos".

In our everyday use of the word, chaos means total disorder. The edge of chaos is not total disorder and not total confusion. It is a phase transition as a system moves from stability to instability. The instability of the edge of chaos is therefore contained: bounded instability. It is a mixture of both order and disorder from which new forms and new ways of behaving emerge and unfold in both uncertain yet analogous ways, in an erratic yet habitual manner.

This edge of chaos is a far-from-equilibrium state, a phase transition between total order – ossification – and total disorder – disintegration – and yet this is potentially a highly creative space, one from which new forms and new order spontaneously emerge from the interactions of agents in the systems. In our everyday world, the interactions are the conversations which we have with each other, hence the importance of relating to one another in the workplace.

At the edge of chaos, self-organisation is productive and creative as new forms and new strategies emerge. We cannot organise this self-organisation. For example, we cannot take people to the edge of chaos. They spontaneously choose to do so or not, and of course, the project leader is part of this process, not outside it.

We co-create the future although we are not in control: the importance of "taking part"

The key question for all of us in a work organisation from a complexity perspective is: to what extent are we participating in the process, to what extent are we attempting to influence the future through taking part? Complexity shows us that we are all interrelated, and as all parts are connected and affect each other, we cannot as individuals not take part, we cannot not participate. Our everyday decisions, choices, actions and non-actions all have an effect. So, although we do not and cannot control an unknown and unknowable future, we are the co-creators of our future. We can and do influence it. Hence, as will be discussed more thoroughly later on, we need to learn to take responsibility for our participation. When things do not work out the way we would like them to do, the question is to ask ourselves what we did/did not do which led to this outcome for we are all responsible.

Emergent strategies: the importance of conversations and relationships

From what we know about complex work organisations, strategies emerge from the messiness and the chaos of our everyday world. What we have to do simply surfaces, in what writers about complexity call "order for free". Out of the disorder and chaotic nature of life and work, order and new patterns emerge. These materialize from the interactions which we have with each other. Complexity theory draws our attention to the ordinary in organisations, to the micro level of everyday life. We learn from the findings of people working in that field that it is from our everyday interactions and conversations with each other that our strategies take shape. It is in the everyday contact with others that the strategies we need to adopt emerge. Hence, it is crucial for us to look at the type of conversations which people have with each other, because the quality of our interactions will affect the quality of our strategies. Hence, relationships between people in the workplace have an important bearing on the accomplishment of the task at hand. Developing good relationships and encouraging conversations between people in an informal manner become the most important interventions for managers and project leaders.

Other useful strategies in the light of an uncertain future: short-term planning and continuous monitoring

What we now know is that all long-term planning is problematic. However, the degree of uncertainty is greatly lessened in the short term. Therefore, wise managers engage seriously in short-term planning. This is because it takes a certain length of time for the impact of a change to be experienced within the system.

As there is still a degree of uncertainty even with short-term planning, it is crucial that very close monitoring take place and that the findings from this monitoring activity are constantly fed back into the system. Effective and discerning managers engage in this continuous monitoring almost intuitively. They are aware of what is going on and often work by what is known as "managing by walking about". Constant monitoring occurs through observation, listening to people, noticing important signs, taking note of feelings and emotions as well as documenting more objective indicators. Monitoring needs also to occur in a more systematic fashion. A vital message, therefore, is that close monitoring, feedback and regularly reviewed short-term strategies are crucial if we wish to manage effectively in conditions of complexity and uncertainty.

Implications and useful strategies

Perceptive project leaders are at all times flexible. Rigidity, set procedures and set standards will not be useful when we are dealing with uncertainty and complexity. We may be guided by principles. For example, this book aims to provide some principles. But no one can tell us in advance exactly what to do. Using principles which seem to work, we have to continuously create and innovate and in so doing we come up with new principles and new guidelines. In this way, we become engaged in a continuous learning process. The thriving organisation is in a state of ceaselessly unlearning old ways and learning new ones, of giving up old patterns and engaging in the creation of new forms. Effective individuals engage in the same process.

The "hidden" order in the disorder of chaos is useful to us in practical terms. These patterns are valuable in guiding our work, but we need to ensure that we do not use simple cause-and-effect models. We rarely, if ever, can say that doing X will cause Y to occur. Life in work organisations is much more complex than this. Therefore, in the face of chaos we have to accept complexity, face it squarely and not simply wish that it will go away – that is the disorder part of chaos. We also have to recognise patterns to guide our actions – the order part of chaos.

Staff meetings in this project are always unpleasant and difficult to manage. People arrive late or do not send their apologies when they do not attend. The atmosphere is disagreeable. Staff either remain very quiet or denigrate everything which the manager says. Often personal attacks are made by members of staff, sometimes aimed at the manager or sometimes aimed at colleagues. Aisha, who is the deputy director of the project, is particularly difficult and is often the one to attack the manager.

The pattern of difficult staff meetings suggests that there are problems in this project. The wise manager notices this pattern and attempts to deal with it. There is rarely a simple cause and effect when we deal with people. Therefore the "problem" is probably a complex one and the complexity of this issue will have to be addressed. We would need more information to know how to deal with this situation. The example could have a multitude of "causes", for example, it could suggest that Aisha was a difficult and unpleasant colleague, that the staff is demotivated, that there is poor leadership, that there are hidden organisational problems, that there is inadequate communication, that decisions are taken in a top-down manner and as a result staff sabotage the system, etc. In reality, there are probably several issues which are interconnected and all these would have to be addressed. The effective manager faces complexity and does not search for clear prescriptions. The world we deal with is much more complex than the simple cause-and-effect picture which linear models suggest.

The existence of patterns in work organisations means that project leaders have some sources of certainty – not everything is uncertain. In work, as in the wider world, there is both certainty and uncertainty at the same time.

Activity 1.2
– What are the recognisable patterns in your project?
– How useful are these in guiding your work?

Paradox is a characteristic of the chaotic edge

At the chaotic edge, opposites exist at the same time. As mentioned above, there is both order and disorder, both certainty and uncertainty. Paradox is the norm. This means that conflicting tendencies are present simultaneously. This is known as the "both... and..." world as opposed to a black-and-white "either... or..." world. In complexity, there are no simple answers, as the "either... or..." model, which guides linear thinking, implies. Instead, we find different shades of grey. With paradox, there are no straightforward answers. A dilemma can be resolved, as there we are dealing with an "either ... or ..." situation. But there is not a definite answer to a paradox which cannot be totally resolved as two contradictory features are present at the same time. This contradiction produces tension which potentially can be very creative. For example, work organisations need to have some stability and they need to change. We have divisions of labour in a work unit, which leads to segments in the shape of different departments, sections, teams, etc., and we also require integration for the organisation to have a cohesive identity.

This international NGO has been growing in size for a number of years. The headquarters, based in London, now oversees a huge number of projects. People want more autonomy, especially those who work at field level. The NGO decides to decentralize and gives much autonomy to designated regions. This time, staff are unhappy for they say that they have lost their sense of identity. They complain that the top managers used to know what was happening on the ground and it was easy to communicate with them. The NGO is pulled back towards more centralization. When this occurs, people start to complain again that there is not enough autonomy and that they do not like the top-down directives from headquarters.

Here we have a classic problem which organisations often attempt to resolve from an "either… or…" stance instead of facing the paradox which is present. This is the paradox of integration and autonomy. Generally, people want both. They want to belong, they yearn for a sense of identity, they wish for good coordination between departments and, at the same time, they desire discretion, autonomy and the freedom to make their own decisions. People want clear guidelines from the top and at the same time they object to top-down leadership. They wish to belong to a social group and, at the same time, want to maintain their own individuality. There is always some tension between the needs of the individual and the needs of the wider group: the organisation. At some level we have to face the contradictions. In the example about centralization, a centralized system is a well-integrated system; a move towards decentralization means that integration has been lost, there is now fragmentation and lack of integration. Integration is sought by re-giving more control to the centre and so it goes on.

Wise managers are aware of the irreconcilable tension between centralization and decentralization, between control at the top and control at field level, between a strong sense of identity in a well-integrated organisation and the autonomy of workers and between the needs of the collective and the needs of the individual. These cannot be totally reconciled. But if used astutely, paradox is a great source of creativity. An outcome of this situation is that conflict is inevitable. It is important to be aware that conflict can be useful to work organisations. We have to learn how to handle conflict, so that human beings do not get hurt. But conflict is good for work settings and potentially very creative.

Implications for project leaders

The wise project leader therefore recognises the potentially positive aspect of conflict, which is an opportunity for learning and creativity. She also accepts the paradoxical nature of the world and learns to deal with paradox, e.g., by seeking non-linear models to help her in decision-making. We shall be looking at some of these models in a later chapter.

Activity 1.3

Thinking about your project, what are the elements of paradox which you can identify, what are the contradictions present? How are these contradictions handled at present?

Surviving and thriving at the chaotic edge

The edge of chaos is where we find life, where we find creative ways of dealing with complexity and an unknown and unknowable future. When people self-organise through their interactions and their relationships, they may choose to operate at the edge of chaos. They embrace the messiness and the bounded instability; and they accept paradox and thrive on the creative tension of this paradoxical world. They tolerate the anxiety which comes from taking a step into the future, turning this anxiety into excitement and being able to stay in a far-from-equilibrium space from which new patterns emerge. They engage in the life of the organisation, through relating to each other, influencing the outcomes with their dreams and their aspirations which form the basis of the interactions which they have with others. People and work organisations embracing the "edge of chaos" are no longer searching for set prescriptions, they engage with the present and learn as they go along. They have their dreams and outcomes they would like to attain. But they know that with an uncertain future, no-one can guarantee what the result of their actions will be. They constantly monitor what is going on and change as the need arises. They recognise the importance of processes and are aware that the "people element" is the most significant to the organisation. They engage in constructive conflict and deal with issues until these are resolved. They recognise the cyclical nature of the world with matters getting worse before they get better and then becoming inauspicious again. They do not believe that life and work are one smooth easy path with no problems along the way, but that the path is a tortuous one with good and bad times; this cycle never ceases. Very importantly, they are energised by this phenomenon and thrive by becoming very creative. Consequently, they do not have the utopian dream of a golden, problem-free future which they will one day reach. They acknowledge that this is not so and trust that they will know how to deal with the good times as well as how to handle the bad times ahead which they cannot avoid.

They take full responsibility for what happens to them and do not engage in a fruitless search for others to blame. They are organised and do plan their everyday actions. For the routine part of their work, for administrative and clerical matters, there are rules and procedures, but even these contain flexibility to deal with the unexpected. But they are aware of the parts of their work which cannot be planned in advance. They have ideas about what to do, but these proposals and suggestions are in a constant flux, changing as they learn new things while they proceed. They give up the need to control, accepting that as mere human beings it is not in our power to control the future; at the same time, they trust their own abilities to deal with whatever comes their way. They take full responsibility for what they do and do not do. They are aware that they can influence the future, although they cannot control it. Therefore they take part in the action. They are not tied to a set paradigm, but are prepared to unlearn as the need arises. They are conscious that the most important element in their work is that of relating with one another, thus creating the conditions for creative self-organisation at the edge of chaos with constant learning and perpetual change.

References and further reading

Parker D. and Stacey R. (1994) *Chaos, Management and Economics – the Implications of Non-linear Thinking*, Hobart Paper 125, Institute of Economic Affairs, London.

Stacey R. (1992) *Managing Chaos*, Kogan Page Ltd, London.

Stacey R. (1993) *Strategic Management and Organisational Dynamics*, Pitman Publishing, London.

Chapter 2   Managing complexity – unhelpful and effective strategies

The issue

Dealing with complexity and an uncertain future necessitates developing valuable strategies. This demands a different approach to that advocated by linear management models which accentuate the need for order, stability, logical and rational thinking. From the linear perspective, management is about control. But we cannot control an unknown and unknowable future. Developing the skills we require to deal with complexity and uncertainty makes us feel in charge while accepting that most of the time we are not in control. Anxiety and fear raised by an uncertain complex world may lead individuals and organisations to develop strategies which protect in the short term by allaying anxiety, but which are not creative and useful. However, there are skills and attitudes which we can develop to deal effectively with uncertainty and complexity. We need to learn how to survive and thrive in the messy world we inhabit.

When we do not know what to do in the face of uncertainty and complexity, the functioning of the right brain hemisphere (as opposed to the logical, rational mode of the left brain hemisphere), such as intuition, creativity and the use of imagery, is invaluable.

Protective but uncreative mechanisms

When people encounter uncertainty and complexity and do not have the skills to deal with these, they are inclined to resort to defensive strategies which are attempts to eliminate the underlying fear. These mechanisms serve a purpose in the short term in that people feel better and feel protected. They alleviate our unease and the lack of control we experience, but they are not effective in helping us with the issues and the problems do not go away. Faced with not knowing what to do, many managers and organisations latch on to their favourite mechanisms. This next section will look at some common ones. It is useful to know what these are, so that we can recognise them in ourselves and our projects. We can appreciate what may be happening to people who work with us and be better placed to support them. As project leaders, we need to be alert to what may be going on. More importantly, we can develop better strategies and help those with whom we work to acquire useful and helpful approaches.

Secrecy

Secrecy arises when people do not know what they are doing but pretend that they do know. They engage in various office rituals to keep up the impression that they are in control. Deep down they are anxious and often complain of being stressed and may become ill.

The culture of the organisation often reinforces this secrecy as the belief system is one where managers and project leaders should know what to do and the organisation does not allow for mistakes.

Jennifer was known to be an effective project leader. She worked for an international NGO and had served on several emergency missions. She came across as a competent worker. But Jennifer was often unsure about how to proceed. She dealt with the uncertainty by appearing confident and issuing orders to the team. She often felt unwell and suffered from intense headaches and insomnia, but these symptoms appeared only when she was sent on a mission. Jennifer had never admitted to anyone that she frequently felt unable to cope because the organisation made it clear that it expected project leaders to be competent and resourceful people. She believed that to admit to her feelings would mean that they would no longer employ her and she did appreciate being able to help people in distress.

This international NGO is well known for the emergency work it undertakes. The great majority of workers are very highly stressed. A few engage in effective coping strategies to combat the distress they experience, but they keep this a secret from their colleagues. At the other extreme, some workers are resorting to soft drugs, smoking and alcohol to deal with stress. Most workers are somewhere in between

*the two extremes. Workers faced with appalling conditions feel inade-
quate and often do not know what to do. In private, people admit to
feeling very anxious. But in an organisation which projects an image
of competent workers who are in control of the most dire situations,
people are unable to confess that they are often at a loss. This is the
secret of the organisation. The consequence is that there is a high level
of distress among workers with many in the stage of burn-out.*

Busy-ness

For some people and some organisations, a common strategy is to
engage in busy-ness. People become over-active and move towards
a state of disintegration. The over-activity compensates for the
feelings of being in the dark. People are so active that they do not
have time to engage in the dangerous activity of reflection because
if they did so, they might have to confront the fact that they are totally lost and do not know what to do. This over-activity does produce
some results but the level of productivity is not in relation to the
amount of energy spent. The energy is going mainly into keeping
active.

*Several international NGOs seem to fall into that mould, being con-
stantly overactive with emphasis on action and doing. Many of their
workers are highly stressed. The organisation is in a state of disintegration. The busy-ness escalates as the level of uncertainty and complexity increases. One such organisation describes itself as a "headless chicken going round in circles", a metaphor which graphically
depicts the intense activity and the low level of effective output.*

Paralysis

Other organisations and other people react to not knowing what to
do in just the reverse of busy-ness. This time, we find a sort of paralysis with no real action being undertaken. This shows itself by pro-
crastination. It also reveals itself through endless meetings and committees where people talk and discuss incessantly but nothing or not
very much is actually carried out in practice.

This time the main culprits in low- and middle-income countries appear to be government departments where not very much actually gets done although many meetings are held and a large number of reports are produced. These organisations are in a state of ossification and cannot deal with any sort of change. Their fear leads to paralysis.

Control through the search for set procedures, rules and regulations

In other cases, when confronted by uncertainty and complexity, people attempt to control the uncontrollable. Rigidity is one way of making themselves believe that they are in control. Another practice in organisations is that of producing procedures, rules and regulations in a bid to regulate the unknown and the unknowable. The existence of these rules and procedures comforts people, even if they know that in practice these do not work. Drawing up long-term plans is another means of believing that we are in control, with the underlying assumption being that we can predict what will happen in the future.

A team of community health nurses has been set up to prevent child abuse in a specific geographical area. To some extent their task is an impossible one, but they accept the role. Although they know much about child abuse in the community, this is a very intricate matter and there is always uncertainty in that type of work. In the face of the many ambiguities in their work, they engage in a frantic search for set rules and procedures which they believe will prevent child abuse in the community as long as other professionals follow these procedures rigidly.

Belief in a conspiracy plot

Another way which some organisations deal with the fear raised by uncertainty and complexity is to find a scapegoat to blame. There is sometimes an almost paranoid belief that someone is the cause of their troubles. Here people are reassured by being able to identify as a scapegoat the person or the organisation which is the source of all their problems. It would be too disturbing to accept that what is happening is a result of living in a chaotic and complex world which they cannot control. It is much easier for them to postulate that someone else is inducing what troubles them. At the same time, people do not have to take responsibility for what is happening to them. They can simply accuse someone else. We shall go on to see how disempowering it is to blame others for our ills – even if in some way they may have contributed to our problems.

No one is certain about the future of this project as securing funding is becoming more difficult. The project leader has drawn up a 5-year plan which is approved by the workers. Although the topic is addressed, no-one directly confronts either the very uncertain future which threatens the survival of the project or ways of dealing with this uncertainty. Instead, in staff meetings, people play the "find someone to blame game." They identify three people but the real ogre of the story is the Regional Medical Officer, whom they feel is determined not to support their work although they know that he also is at risk under the financial cuts. Most of the time and energy at staff meetings is spent denigrating the Regional Medical Officer. People come to meetings with stories about him which invariably have the same plot – the Regional Medical Officer as persecutor of yet another victim. Recently there has been much gossip in the organisation about his private life.

Belief in a parent figure

Another unhelpful strategy is the fantasy that there are parent figures somewhere who can step in and help. In this case, people are aware that they do not know what to do but they believe that there is someone, somewhere, who knows what to do and who will be able to save them. Or, at least, the belief is that these others ought to know what to do and should be in control of circumstances. People often attribute almost magical powers to those who are in authority and subsequently blame them for not having those. Politicians are often the targets of this belief and, of course, politicians in return often promise what they cannot possibly provide. In work organisations authority figures are often the victim of these fantasies, and consultants are often called in with the secret wish that they can sort out the problems of the organisation in an almost magical way. When they fail to deliver the magical solutions, they are blamed for the situation in which the organisation finds itself.

This small international NGO is floundering under the weight of the complexity of the projects which they have started all over the world. The future is very uncertain as they do not know from year to year who will support their projects. Political situations in several countries are continuously changing. At regular intervals they call in management consultants whom they hope will be able to sort out all their problems. They employ these consultants on a very short-term basis with no follow-up built in. Each time they are disappointed by the management consultant and move on to someone else. Energy is then spent on blaming the previous consultants for not having helped and the search for a new "saviour" starts all over again.

Fantasy of omnipotence and of perfection: the "playing God" game

Another tactic found in some organisations is the fantasy that they are all-powerful and/or totally perfect. In this world, no human being is either all-powerful or perfect. There is so much which we simply cannot control, including the course of our own lives. For example, some people prefer not to face the only certainty in life that is death itself. But many health professionals are often socialized into believing that they can control dying. In many hospitals, the death of patients is seen as a failure and many health professionals have internalized this view, often unconsciously. When they become managers of projects, they often replicate the same belief system. Some organisations believe that they are totally perfect. In an imperfect world to aim for perfection is highly unrealistic. But the organisation believes that whatever it engages in is the correct thing to do and it also considers itself to have the right answers and solutions to issues.

These organisations fail to learn from what happens to them and are resistant to change. Deep down, however, people do know that they are not omnipotent or perfect; thus there are often high levels of distress among workers.

This NGO works in a variety of countries in both emergency and long-term projects. It deals with a wide range of extreme social problems. There is nothing which it feels it cannot undertake. Whenever there is a new crisis in the world, or a new request for help, it responds and sets up a project. Workers are at first full of enthusiasm but in the long-term they all suffer from high levels of stress and become burnt out. They fail to hear the feedback which local people attempt to give to them because they deem that they do know what to do in most circumstances – although overtly they have a policy of participation by the people they are supposed to serve. The organisational culture reflects the belief that they can shoulder anything which comes their way. This is reflected in the name of the organisation.

Becoming aware of our unhelpful strategies

In an organisation where secrecy reigns, being able to speak out, to talk and to divulge our secrets is a useful first step which is often greeted with relief.

When organisations are overactive, it is valuable to ask whether this busy-ness serves only in hiding people's fears. This type of busy-ness, as described earlier, shows itself by frantic action which does not lead to much in terms of productivity. Furthermore, as we shall discuss later on, healthy organisations have some slack time built in for reflection and creative work. Extreme busy-ness is not very conducive to creativity. If there is no time for quiet work and time for deliberation, schedules have to be altered.

If instead an organisation is in a state of paralysis this also has to be addressed. Constant deliberation about what to do without action does not get a project anywhere.

When the strategy consists of writing up rules, regulations and procedures, people have to ask whether these are actually useful. As we shall go on to see when we discuss decision-making, rules and procedures are only effective in conditions of certainty and where tasks are fairly simple.

In organisations where workers engage in blaming others because of a covert or overt belief that there is some conspiracy against them, they need to recognise how disempowering it is to blame others for what happens to them. This is wasted energy and this energy could be better placed into addressing what it is that the organisation can do which is within its powers.

When the people in an organisation believe in a parent figure who will, it is hoped, one day take care of them and sort out their problems, they are also disempowering themselves. This is a child-like behaviour and like children, people behaving in this way live in the hope that a fairy godmother will come to save them with a magic wand. If we want to be empowered, we have to give up the idea that there are saviours out there who will come and rescue us. Instead, we have to believe that we are quite capable of taking care of ourselves. This is an adult response with us taking responsibility for ourselves. We accept that we cannot foretell the future but we also believe that we have the capabilities to sort out what we will have to do; we do know that human beings possess these capacities. All we have to do is use them.

Dealing with unhelpful strategies: the importance of giving people protective skills

As was mentioned above, unhelpful mechanisms perform a function, at least in the short term. They protect individuals and organisations against the anxiety provoked by chaos, complexity and uncertainty. They are not very effective in the long term, as energy is being devoted to protecting against fear rather than dealing with uncertainty and complexity competently. Therefore, in an ideal world, we would not engage in these unhelpful tactics. We have to recognise what is happening if a work organisation embarks on one or more of these strategies. But it is also important to acknowledge the protective effect of the stratagem. The mechanism is serving a purpose. To encourage people to use effective and positive strategies, they require sufficient skills to be able to deal with complexity. Much of what follows in this book is concerned with these necessary skills. We also have to accept that sometimes not everyone in a work organisation will acquire these skills. It is, however, important for managers and project leaders to have the right attitudes, beliefs and competencies to deal with chaos. They also have to be alert to common unhelpful tactics and to attempt to remedy them. This is when it is important for them to acknowledge that people need the protection afforded by these strategies. To remove them without giving people other means of safety will lead to insurmountable resistance, as people will endeavour at all cost to protect themselves. We see the same pattern of behaviour at an organisational level. As change agents, we have to discover what is useful and positive in the strategies and we cannot expect people to change without providing them with the skills to protect themselves so that they can survive and thrive in a chaotic world. We can work with the strategies used by an organisation as a means to move forward. As an example, in a project which engages in paralysis, we can use the non-action as reflective time to encourage workers to find creative solutions to the issues they face.

Activity 2.1

Reflecting on your work organisation, identify any unhelpful tactics which the organisation employs.

– **How disempowering are these strategies?**
– **What protective function do they serve?**
– **What may be positive about those strategies?**
– **This time, thinking about yourself, are there any unhelpful mechanisms which you use?**
– **What can you do personally to adopt a more positive strategy?**

Positive strategies

To deal effectively with uncertainty and complexity we need to become aware of unhelpful stratagems and to refrain from engaging in those. We also require the attitudes and skills to deal with the anxiety provoked by uncertainty and complexity. An important role for

managers and project leaders is that of dealing effectively with anxiety and to help people – including themselves – to acquire more
useful strategies and develop the skills necessary for the complex
uncertain world. The following chapters will consider the attitudes
and skills more fully. Here, we look at the importance of acknowl-
edging what we do not know and how we have to engage in a thinking mode different to that of the logical, rational part of the brain
when we do not know what to do.

The skills for living and working with complexity and uncertainty

How do we survive and thrive in a chaotic world? Very few of us
have been taught valuable life skills. Yet we acquire them, gleaning
along our life paths these competencies which serve us well in a
chaotic world. Too often, however, it has not been pointed out to us
how effective these life-skills are in our work as managers and as
project leaders. Many of the skills which will be described are those
we have already obtained along the way to where we are now. But
we have to become aware of how crucial they are in managing
projects.

Linear traditional models of management identify a different set of
skills. According to the old paradigm, a manager functions in a very
logical manner. The most valued skill is that of rational thinking and
the manager is to work in an objective way.

The chapter on decision-making will show that there are many
instances when we do need to draw on clear analytical reasoning. A
rational and logical mind is useful in conditions of certainty. When we
are sure of something and there appears to be a simple causal link, then
this type of thinking is the most useful. This applies to many purely
technical matters in the professional world this applies. However, we
have to be aware that what helps us in the technical aspects of our work
may not be at all helpful when applied to managing a project. When
we are dealing with complexity and uncertainty we have to draw on
very disparate abilities. The new approach demands unconventional
and unusual competencies.

Admitting to not-knowing

In the face of the anxiety which most of us experience in chaotic situations, the most positive strategy is simply to accept our feelings and discover what we need to do. Facing our fear is very liberating. Just to admit that we do not know what to do and that we are anxious about the "not-knowing" constitutes a major breakthrough. This very simple step actually frees us from the negative conditions which we attribute to fear and anxiety. But more importantly, it seems crucial to acknowledge that it is quite acceptable to admit to not knowing and to being anxious, because when we do so, paradoxically we are better able to find useful strategies in the midst of uncertainty and complexity.

In many work organisations, people find this easy step to be insurmountable. Yet leading managers and management consultants have no problems admitting to not knowing. Therefore, it is vital for organisations to allow such statements to be made. Those who have tried this step often find that what appears to be a chasm is less daunting when they admit to not knowing. Breaking through the wall of secrecy is crucial. Therefore, a critical strategy is just to admit that we do not know.

Activity 2.2

In your own work organisation, how easy is it for you to admit to not knowing what to do when this is your personal experience?
If you are unable to admit to not-knowing, what are the factors which make it difficult for you to do so? Differentiate between organisational factors and personal ones.

Knowing what to do when we do not know what to do

Writers on complexity point out that the leaders of the future are people who know what to do when they do not know what to do. This sentence probably needs to be read twice to make sense, but this is a significant message for anyone wishing to be a successful project leader.

Faced with uncertainty, complexity, ambiguities and paradox, the logical mind comes to a stop as it functions in an analytical way, moving from step to step. This we cannot do when there are no clear steps along the way. We then feel "stuck", unable to act and plainly not knowing what to do. Most of us at this stage are seized by fear, consciously or unconsciously. When we become anxious we tend on the whole to perceive this as an uncomfortable episode. Sometimes we are not consciously aware of the underlying fear and we find ourselves in a state of mild anxiety or restlessness. Our work suffers, in that, despite our efforts, we do not seem to be getting anywhere. This is the time when we are likely to resort to our favourite unhelpful strategies as described earlier in this chapter. As already stated, a crucial first step is simply to admit to not knowing. Much of what follows in this chapter and subsequent ones are ideas for knowing what to do when we do not know what to do.

The importance of action when we do not know what to do

When we are working in conditions of certainty we can plan and then act. The old paradigm of management relies on this underlying notion as was discussed in the previous chapter. From this perspective what we have to do is simply to produce clear plans with clear steps of how to proceed. In conditions of certainty or relative certainty this is a very useful model. For our every-day affairs, whether in our personal lives or at work, we rely on this pattern. Therefore, when we are dealing with the every-day routine and with certainty, plans are extremely valuable. When we talk of being organised, this is often what we have in mind. For example, a well-kept diary is a useful tool for project leaders. Managers need to be well organised in their daily work. This is the "order", the "stability" in the midst of chaos because, remember, as we have seen in the previous chapter, the chaotic edge is both orderly and disorderly. In the same way, there are certain ways of carrying out simple activities and we write up the best procedure and follow this carefully. Unless conditions change, this plan will serve us well. So, for what is uncomplicated, what is routine and what is certain, a good plan followed by action is the way to proceed and we can have clear systems to help us. However, in the case of uncertainty and complexity the model just outlined plainly does not work.

Before reading on, you might like to attempt the following activity:

Activity 2.3

It is early evening and you are lost in the middle of the countryside. You do not know exactly where you are, although you believe that there is a large town not too far away. There are no road signs, no indication of where you are and no houses in sight. It will soon be dark and you do not want to spend the night in this deserted place. What do you do?

This is an imaginary situation and there are many different answers to what can be done. In real life and in conditions of uncertainty in our project there are also many different possible answers. However, the previous model of writing out a plan and then following the plan is not feasible. Faced with uncertainty, we cannot plan. Although with this fictitious activity there were several possible solutions, there is a common pattern to the many answers. In this case, we need to act first. If we want to get out of the situation we have to do something. What we then discover is that in situations where complexity and uncertainty are present the reverse of the usual planning model applies. We cannot plan and then act. We have to act first. In so doing we will learn something. As we learn we can start to plan. Therefore the model is reversed. Consequently, a very useful strategy when we do not know what to do is simply to do something, just anything, for as we do so, we will start a learning process and this learning process will be our guide.

Different modes of thinking: left brain hemisphere vs right brain hemisphere

Although what I present here is highly simplified, we do know that the two hemispheres of the brain are concerned with very different functions. The left brain, which deals with language and with words, is also the main centre of logical, rational and analytical styles of thinking. The right hemisphere, which is concerned with imagery, stories and metaphors, is involved with intuition, inventiveness and originality. It also sees the whole, therefore it is holistic in approach, while the left hemisphere is more concerned with the parts. To manage well, we require both sides to be functioning adequately. Unfortunately, many of us have been encouraged to use and develop our left brain hemisphere, usually through the formal educational system which emphasises this type of thinking, to the detriment of the right brain mode of operating.

The following is a generalisation but it is possibly fair to say that Western societies give higher status to left brain thinking. Many Eastern countries and countries of the South have traditionally favoured right brain thinking, a situation often altered by the formal educational system, which is usually modelled on Western countries. What we need to do is redress the balance and give due consideration to both types of thinking and reasoning as we require both for decision-making.

Usefulness of the right brain hemisphere

When issues are complex and there is a high level of uncertainty, right brain functioning can be very valuable. It is of great help when we feel "stuck" and cannot move on. The logical mind is not effective in these situations as there are no clear steps to follow. We simply do not know what these steps are. We shall look at some of the useful functions of the right brain in this section, particularly the use of intuition, imagery and metaphors.

The importance of "slack" quiet times

Before we look at some "right brain" modes, it is important to point out that these should not be seen as mere techniques to be used in a rational, logical fashion. Generally, formal education systems not only favour the logical mode but also give high value to quick thinking; some authors refer to this as "hare" brain, referring to the well-known story of the hare and the tortoise where the hare puts emphasis on speed but is overtaken by the slow tortoise. This little story is an apt analogy for the type of "thinking" which is more likely to help us when we do not know what to do in the face of uncertainty and complexity. The slow tortoise is often what is necessary. Emphasis on time, on rapidity and speed means that many of us no longer value quiet times and time to stare and reflect. "Tortoise mind" (Claxton, 1998) demands a different relationship to time. In the busy-ness of many work organisations, time for reflection and for engaging with our "unconscious" right brain function is simply not there. Therefore, we need to learn to treasure silence, to engage in tortoise fashion proceeding slowly and ensuring that there are these quiet periods in our lives.

Intuition

Intuition is difficult to define; it is not the opposite of rational think-ing but something which is different from the rational, logical style of thinking. Writing about management, Agor (1989) and Senge (1992) point out how important intuition is for decision-making. Agor (1989) argues that there are many situations – where things are not known and are complex and uncertain – where intuition is either the only mode or a better one than the logical, rational mode of deci-sion-making. He believes that intuition is a crucial skill for leaders and managers which can lead to increased productivity, both for the individual and the organisation. Senge notes that in recent years many research studies have pointed out how important intuition is to managers and leaders, as this is the mode used by many leaders when dealing with complex issues, where they rely on their "hunch-es" and on analogies to decide how to proceed in complex and uncertain situations. Intuition is a skill, which until recently has been generally ignored in work organisations, with the over-reliance on the linear paradigm which favours the logical, rational and ana-lytical mode of thinking.

Intuition is a holistic mode of decision-making, a way of knowing where we are unable to explain why we know. Somehow we see the whole of what is bothering us. Sometimes we may have been "stuck" for a period of time, unable to find a solution to our problem, and then we get an insight about how to proceed. At other times we immediate-ly have a feeling that we should pursue a certain route. We cannot usu-ally explain why we should choose this particular path. We just know that this is what we ought to do. There is a strong feeling of knowing without being able to provide the usual logical explanations. When intuition is at play and we find explanations, these interpretations are often an after-thought, a means of persuading others that our idea is a good one. Intuitive thinking often appears "out of the blue", with no logical steps leading to it. Intuitive thoughts tend to come as flashes, through emotions or through a bodily feeling that this is the right path. People refer to a feeling, a sensation in their body, often at the level of the stomach or abdomen, hence intuitive thought is commonly referred to as a "gut feeling." People will say "I have a gut feeling that this is what we have to do". It has been found by organisational researchers (see suggested reading at the end of this chapter) that top executives who have to take crucial decisions in contexts of uncertainty, ambiguity and complexity resort to their intuition. However, as most of us live and work in a culture where predominance is given to the logical, rational and analytical way of thinking, these top executives rarely admit to those around them that this is how they take their major decisions. They go into board meetings after having mapped out a logical analysis to convince others that their ideas are important enough to be adopted. They keep their use of intuition a secret, for fear of not being taken seriously in a world which does not value intuitive thinking. More importantly, these top executives report that things go wrong when they disregard their intuitive ideas. When what they have in mind works, it is inevitably because they followed their intuition (Agor, 1989).

However, intuition by itself is not sufficient. To survive and thrive in chaotic conditions we need to draw on both our intuition and on logical thinking, a point which I shall discuss more fully later on. However, intuition is crucial to managers to help them take decisions; not least because it is important for managers to be able to see the "big picture" in an organisation and intuition is a holistic type of decision-making.

Developing intuition

Like other skills, intuition has to be developed. If we do not use it, it does not serve us well when we require it. The more we use intuition in our decision-making, the better it will be in guiding us when we require it.

Negative emotions such as fear and anger, too much stress and wanting something too much all get in the way of exercising intuition.

Being generally well in all spheres, i.e., the physical, emotional, mental and spiritual elements of life, is therefore useful to us in our decision-making. A first step is to review our level of self-care and how we ensure our general health and well-being. Second, it is crucial to believe that intuition is valuable, as without this basic belief our intuition will fail to help us. Third, we have to practice using it and thus enhance our intuitive abilities.

Writers on the use of intuition in work organisations recommend the following to develop our intuitive capabilities:

- Meditation.
- Relaxation on a regular basis.
- Keeping a record of hunches and noting which ones prove to be accurate and which ones do not; this gives valuable information about what works for us, and also about what is blocking the flow of intuition. An important aim of this exercise is to learn to distinguish intuitive thoughts from those provoked by anxiety or by wishful thinking.
- Having a notepad available at all times to jot down any ideas, hunches and flashes of insight and following these up, i.e., making sure that we capture these ideas and use them.
- Guided imagery, use of visualization (see a later section in this chapter) and analysing night and day dreams.
- Developing a relaxed and a positive frame of mind.
- Working informally and in a fun manner.
- Having some regular spiritual and/or philosophical nourishment.
- Sleeping on a problem, or taking time off to relax and let go of the problem.

Activity 2.4

- **Assess how good you are at developing your intuition.**
- **What steps can you take to ensure the improvement of your intuitive faculties?**

Creative managers use their intuition first, then they engage in left brain hemisphere activity to translate their ideas into practice. For innovative ideas, then, we are using both right and left brain hemi-spheres. We follow up intuitive ideas by testing their feasibility. We then engage in logical thinking, working out finances and other resource implications as well as organising how to put our ideas into practice in the real world. Any innovative process brings together the use of right and left brain hemispheres.

The creative process

The creative process often starts by a mainly left brain hemisphere activity, such as that of gathering and analysing information and try-ing to make sense of this material in a logical way. Then, very often, we reach a stage of feeling "stuck" where we do not make any progress and we feel confused and frustrated. Many people become so overwhelmed by anxiety at this stage that they give up. However, if we accept this stage we can become very creative. Note once again that acceptance of not knowing what to do is of great signifi-cance. That first step of simply embracing this frustration of not being able to progress is very important as it is often part of the cre-ative process. As we know from complexity theory, creativity comes from far-from-equilibrium conditions and our confusion and per-plexity are just this potentially very creative far-from-equilibrium state. For us to become creative, we have to accept to live in that state of chaos and not retreat to stability. Right brain hemisphere functions become valuable here. This is a period of incubation where we keep on working on the problem at a subconscious or unconscious level. From this incubation period, we gain an insight: what is referred to as the "aha" experience in learning. We often make this sound "ah! ah!" having suddenly discovered how we are to proceed. After gaining this insight, we engage primarily in left brain hemisphere functions to work out what resources we require to put our ideas into practice. The final stage of implementation is very much a combination of both left and right brain functions.

   Yes, the creative process does include these phases. But this is not the whole story. The above description, as for most narratives using verbal language as a medium, is a predominantly left brain hemisphere activity. It is difficult to translate accurately the functioning of the right brain using left brain terminologies. I am very aware of this problem in the process of writing this book. So much of what is very important is missed out. But for this book to be published, I also have to resort to what top executives have to do in the boardrooms: use left brain techniques. A book about managing projects in low- and middle-income countries with only stories, parables, metaphors and imagery would probably not be published and you may be reluctant to read it. Therefore, to return to the description of the creative process, this is a linear narrative recounted with hindsight. Although we often can recognise the phases described, these are but the patterns of the chaotic edge. The reality is much more untidy, perplexing and confusing than what I have just described. At times we move from one phase to another, at other times they seem to be happening simultaneously and they do not follow the clear step-by-step outline that I have provided. So the creative process which emerges from the chaotic edge is one where eventually we recognise figures and patterns, but where for a major part of the time we find ourselves in the throes of bewilderment, disorientation and confusion. There are many unknown as well as recognisable known patterns. As for anything to do with complexity, there are elements of instability and of the unknown and components of stability and of the known. What I have described is simply the latter, i.e., the recognisable patterns to which we have to cling, so as to make sense of the unknown and the uncertain. We have to remember that the point of being "stuck", i.e., the dead end which we meet, is part of the creative process. For many people, this stage is emotionally upsetting. It is crucial that we learn to accept this phase and that we stay with it. We do feel lost but it is critical to stay there – until we reach the "aha" experience, until insight comes our way. This is when reflective quiet times are most useful to us. Occupying ourselves with non-purposeful activities is a useful strategy for dealing with that space. In this way, we make ourselves available for insight to come our way. This is the time to engage in tasks such as filing, tidying up cupboards and drawers, sorting out our offices, etc. At the personal level, it involves the ability to be comfortable with wilderness, with uncertainty. It requires the capacity to go into unknown places where there is no clear understanding.

As with intuition, we need to develop our creative abilities. The following exercise provides some means of doing so.

Activity 2.5

Developing creativity

- **Do something new or different on a regular basis.**
- **Defend your creative time – ensure that you have some quiet space for reflection, and quiet times when you are not disturbed.**
- **Develop your ability to focus, for example, by meditation and by using all senses: smelling, looking, listening, feeling, tasting.**
- **Become responsive to what goes on; make a habit of developing alternatives.**
- **Be wild, do not censor ideas – have as many wild ideas as possible.**
- **Make a start, do not procrastinate.**
- **When you are asked for your judgment and your opinion about something, make a habit of starting with a positive point.**
- **When an idea or suggestion does not appeal to you, do not reject it straight away or do not dismiss it totally. Instead, consider whether there are components which may be useful.**
- **Whenever a negative event occurs, find out what is positive about this occurrence and ascertain how you can create opportunities from this adverse experience. Make a habit of discovering the positive side of everyone and everything.**
- **Ensure that you have at least two or more answers to any problem – generate alternatives rather than the "correct" solution.**
- **Question so-called facts.**
- **Become a risk taker.**
- **Protect your creative ideas from the judgment of others.**

Activity 2.6

Looking at the above list of suggestions, make up your own personal action plan to develop your creativity which is conducive to your own personal and work circumstances.
Decide how often and how you are going to review your action plan.

Activity 2.7

Have some creative time built into your work organisation and in meetings, which is separate from structured time, where judgment is not allowed – to protect the creative ideas which emerge.

Organisational factors facilitating the use of intuition and creativity

We know that organisations can block or facilitate the flow of intuition and creativity. The culture of the organisation is an important one in that if there is much rigidity and inflexibility and mistakes are not allowed, people's creativity and intuition will not flourish. From the research which has been undertaken in work organisations it seems that a casual, informal and relaxed atmosphere, where the emphasis is to see work as fun, is very conducive to right brain functioning. The physical layout, the clothes people wear and the colour schemes also appear important. Cooperation between colleagues is vital for group creativity. In organisations where there is much competition between people, leading to destructive conflict at the interpersonal level based on envy and jealousy, group creativity does not flourish. Good interactions based on respectful relationships encourage self-organisation at the edge of chaos which leads to creative outputs. When communication is effective, based on dialogue with emphasis on listening to others, we can engage in constructive conflict which is valuable for creativity.

Keeping the child in us alive: having fun at work

Being creative involves being childlike, because young children who have not yet been crippled by the adult world are extremely creative. Playfulness is an important part of being innovative and creative. Too often, work organisations do not allow this state of playfulness. Work needs to be fun. As we enjoy what we are doing, we become energised and motivated and we engage with our innate creativity.

Images and metaphors

Imagination is a crucial aspect of the creative process and Einstein believed that intuition, inspiration and imagination were more important than knowledge. Senge (1992) points out that there are many ways of working with our subconscious mind, with imagery and visualization being powerful modes. In developing our creativity we can make use of both our conscious and subconscious mind. Right brain functions such as the use of imagery, pictures, metaphors and symbols are useful ways of making sense of complexity. It seems that many successful people in various spheres of life – the arts, sports and business – use imagery. Imagery and metaphors can be particularly useful at the beginning of a project to enable us to visualise in our imagination what the end product will be like. We can also use it to guide us during a project. We can explore in our mind's eye different strategies and get a picture of what they will lead to. Highly creative people have a clear image in their imagination of what they want to achieve before they start and they are also very good at finishing what they have started. Average people are more likely to complete what they have started if they have in their mind's eye an image of finishing the task. Therefore, a useful device for project leaders is simply that of imagining that they have successfully completed their project.

Creating the image in our imagination is a powerful way of enabling us to make it happen. Paradoxically, success ensues when we expect the outcome to occur while at the same time letting go of the need for the outcome to materialize. By intending, we focus on making things happen, and by letting go, we acknowledge that we do not have total control in this world. If our desired outcome does not come to fruition, we accept that this is not the end of the world, in which case we figure out alternatives. An acceptance that if we do not have our desired outcome, at some level it is not meant for us, enables us to see the positives in the so-called negative events in life.

Having a positive image is crucial to our work. For example, if project leaders and managers do not possess an image of themselves as being successful, attending training courses and reading books such as this one to improve their managerial skills will not help. A prerequisite to being a successful project leader is to hold such a positive image of oneself. Our images of the world are powerful ways of defining reality for us. When we change the image – when we change the story – reality changes, and we will re-address this important issue later on when we look at the change process. Metaphors are another means of using imagery. A metaphor is a figure of speech which often has a very profound meaning. In an earlier example in which we encountered the very busy NGO where people were highly stressed, the metaphor which was used by workers to depict the organisation was one of a "headless chicken running round in circles". Of course, this very negative image was not helping the efforts of people in the organisation. In a later chapter, we shall explore how we can help people find more suitable and positive metaphors by encouraging them to change the stories they live by. Here, we need to note the power of imagery, of symbols and of metaphors in guiding us. A simple way of improving our work is simply to change the image.

Activity 2.8

Close your eyes and relax. Picture yourself as a successful project leader – where are you what are you wearing, what do you look like, what are your feelings, how do you feel about yourself, who is with you, etc.?
Play with this image and think about how you can use what you discover in your everyday work. You might like to draw this picture.

Activity 2.9

Before you start a project (or anything else), carry out the following exercise:
Close your eyes and relax, imagine that you have successfully completed the project; it is the end and everything has worked out very well. Get a clear picture of this success story, describe to yourself what it looks like, what it feels like, what you can hear, smell and see; how does your body feel?

Then work out how you arrived from where you are to-day to this
wonderful ending. How did you get there, what were the important
steps, what proved to be crucial for this successful ending?
You might like to make some notes at this stage.
Next, imagine that you are at the end of your project but this time
it is not at all successful. – As in the first part of this exercise note
everything you can about this picture and work out how it is that
things did not work out.
(Adapted from Glouberman, 1990; see recommended reading at
the end of this chapter.)

References and suggested reading

Agor Weston H. (ed.) (1989) *Intuition in Organizations*, Sage,
London.

Claxton G. (1998) *Hare Brain, Tortoise Mind*, Fourth Estate Ltd,
London.

Glouberman D. (1990) *Life Choices and Life Changes through
Imagework – The Art of Developing Personal Vision*, Unwin Hyman,
London.

Henry J. (ed.) (1991) *Creative Management*, Sage, London.

Senge P.M. (1992) *The Fifth Discipline*, Century Business, London.

Chapter 3   Decision-making in the face of complexity and an unknown future

The issue

As we live and work in a complex and uncertain world, the traditional models of decision-making based on rational and logical thinking are not always helpful. We require new models and this chapter considers some useful ones.

Appropriateness of the manner of decision-making

The traditional paradigm of management assumes that we deal with certainty and relative simplicity most of the time in work organisations. From this perspective, there is one correct answer when we are taking decisions. We arrive at this solution by considering the facts, the data and all the information we have and in the light of these, we use a rational and logical mode of thought to reach an outcome. Decision-making is seen here as a relatively objective exercise. The discussion so far has pointed out the inadequacies of this paradigm when we are confronted by complexity and uncertainty. At times, it is appropriate to take decisions according to the logical rational mode. But this is not always helpful. We go on now to look at a model which helps us in determining what type of decision-making we require for different circumstances. This next model has evolved from the work of many authors and the discussion which follows has been adapted from Stacey (1993) (see suggested reading list at the end of this chapter).

To identify which manner of decision-making we need, we have to analyse the activities of a project in two different dimensions: first, the objectives of the activity, i.e., the desired end-product, and second, the means – the "how-to" of the activities, i.e., the process involved in achieving the outcome.

Agreed objectives and known means: logical rational models

When the means are clear and the objectives agreed by all concerned, we can use the model proposed by the traditional linear paradigm. Here, we do know what is the best way of carrying out something, and we all agree about what the end product ought to be. So, we are dealing by and large with certainty and relative simplicity. In this instance, we are able to plan and then to act according to that plan. Many purely technical tasks and activities come into that category. We can set rules and procedures and train workers to carry out these activities in a step-by-step way. In this case, there are definite answers. We evaluate these activities by considering how well people are adhering to these agreed procedures. We can simply write these rules and instruct workers to follow them.

Verity is in charge of immunisation for the province. It is important to maintain a "cold chain" from the arrival of the vaccines by air from Europe to the most remote and distant villages in the area, as some of the vaccines deteriorate rapidly if they are stored above a certain temperature. Of course, everyone agrees that the vaccines should be efficacious when they are given to the children who live in this region and Verity knows how this should be done. This is a standard practice taught to health professionals during their training in primary health care. Verity writes the procedures for the region and makes sure that people along the line understand these procedures and maintain them. Her monitoring activity consists of ensuring that the procedures are being followed by everyone involved.

Therefore, when there is agreement about objectives and we know how to do something, the rational, logical step-by-step model advocated by the traditional model of management does work and is the style of decision-making to be used. Many professionals have been primarily trained in this model of decision-making. For many technical decisions, this is an appropriate model. But when we are dealing with management issues, many of the activities we engage in do not belong to that category.

Activity 3.1

Think through the activities which you undertake in your project. Identify which ones come under the category just described, i.e., where we know how to carry out the work and where there is agreement about the objectives.

Write out rules, regulations, procedures and blueprints for these activities.

Certainty about means and conflict about outcomes: politicking

In this category of activities, we do know what to do but people disagree about the outcomes, i.e., there is certainty about the means but there is conflict about the end results. The method of decision-making here is one of politicking, i.e., political ways of decision-making.

To ensure that good-quality family planning service is given to the villagers in this district, multi-disciplinary teams have been set up and part of their brief is to ensure that people from the local community are involved. The doctors and the nurses are determined to reduce the birth rate. The social workers and the community workers, as well as many of the women from the local villages, do not agree that reducing the birth rate should be the objective of a family planning service. They believe that the purpose of such a service is that of providing more choices to women about their bodies and their lives. Some of the religious groups oppose family planning. The traditional healers in the area are ambivalent about the service. The village chiefs are quite keen to have the family planning project and tend to side with the health workers. But they want this project to thrive for other reasons; the villages are given incentives by the international drug companies marketing some of these products. Some of the health workers are unaware of the motivation of the chiefs and believe that they too want the birth rate reduced. They do not know how active some of these drug companies have been in the area.

In such a situation where there is disagreement about the outcome of an activity, project leaders and managers have to engage in political activity. Any decision taken will be a result of these political dealings. The skills required are interpersonal ones: assertive communications, how to manage conflict and confrontation, understanding the dynamics of groups and how to negotiate. The name of the game is that of knowing how to deal with power struggles. We cannot proceed in a clear, step-by-step, logical manner, but have to be prepared for unevenness of progress and uncertainty about what will happen and we also have to face very complex situations. Evaluation here consists not only of measuring outcomes but also of how successful we are at achieving our objectives and reviewing the quality of the processes we adopt; how good are we at the skills required for political decision-making?

Activity 3.2

List the activities which belong to that category from your own project.

– **What type of political activities do you undertake?**
– **How good are your skills for engaging in political decision-making?**
– **How would you rate yourself as a negotiator?**

Agreed objectives and unclear means: intuition and trial and error

This category of activities concerns those where we agree about the objectives but the means are complex, unclear, uncertain and unpredictable.

Caroline is in charge of disability projects for two districts in the region. The most important aim of these projects is that of changing the attitude of people towards the disabled and to have the disabled fully integrated in the socio-economic life of this area. Everyone in the project agrees that this is a worthy outcome. However, how to do so is much more problematic. What works in a village does not work some-

where else and project leaders are having to invent new ways of persuading people to change their attitude all the time.

The example above is one where there is agreement about the outcome. But how to obtain the outcome remains very difficult, complex and perplexing. Many managerial tasks are in that category. An example would be that of team-building. Most managers would like to have an effective team, working cohesively together, where people are respected and supported and with creative, constructive conflict occurring; most employees agree that this is a good thing. But the path to get there is full of problems. We may have principles to guide us (the patterns in the midst of chaos), but we need to re-invent, re-create, think fast on our feet each time we deal with these issues. Here, the method of decision-making is that of intuition, where we are guided by our gut feelings. We follow our intuition and test the feasibility of what it tells us to do through trial and error. We have to take risks, as whatever we decide is to some extent a step into the unknown. Furthermore, we never know in advance whether our bright ideas will work or not. We have to engage in constant monitoring, documenting the process and continuously asking the question "is it working?" This close and ceaseless monitoring is critical as we may have taken the wrong step. Only experience will tell. If we have taken an inappropriate decision, we have to stop and start all over again. We must not wait too long to monitor the feasibility of our ideas as the consequences could be disastrous. Therefore we deal with the short term because the long term is too unpredictable and uncertain. Thus we closely monitor the effect of our decision to ensure that we have taken the correct one, otherwise we have to re-think and start again. Our intuition is our best guide for this category of decision-making.

Activity 3.3

– **Which of the activities in your project belong to this section?**
– **How have you used your intuition?**
– **How do you monitor the decisions you take?**
– **How can you improve on taking intuitive decisions?**
– **What steps do you need to take to ensure that you engage in continuous and close monitoring of this type of decision?**

Conflict about objectives and unclear means: keeping close to the user, politicking, intuition and trial and error

The fourth category, includes those activities where there is disagreement about outcomes and the means are complex and uncertain. All truly developmental and educational work comes into that category as well as many managerial activities, especially the issues which concern people. We have to engage in a dialogue with others about the outcomes; these change all the time and the means to reach our outcomes are also very complicated. There are no blueprints for this type of work, and step-by-step plans are not at all useful. Here, we combine the skills of politicking with those of intuition and trial and error. Useful advice is to be very close to the users, i.e., to engage in continuous exchange with the users of our services as the work is mainly concerned with the process. Monitoring and evaluation is about documenting the quality of this process and ensuring that we are vigilant as to what our users wish from us. In these situations, the process is in effect the outcome as we are discovering as we go along and it is our way of operating which is the most important.

Rebecca is a community development worker. The aim of the project is to encourage the development of the community. For the success of this project, it is crucial to ensure the full participation of as many people as possible from the localities. Rebecca soon discovers that different groups have very diverse ideas about what is involved in community development. Her colleagues also have dissimilar perspectives. The aims of this project are open-ended and change all the time. One has to be creative and innovative. Rebecca uses her intuition to guide her and finds herself involved much of the time in politicking.

Activity 3.4

– **Do you have any activities in your project which come under this category?**
– **How do you deal with these activities?**

The above model identifies and categorises the different types of activities in which we may be engaged in a project and distinguishes the styles of decision-making and the skills we require to deal with these diverse activities. Other general models may be useful in taking decisions in a complex world where the future is both unknown and unknowable, but we need to remember that, unlike the rational logical mode of thinking which comes up with one best solution, these approaches will not yield a definite answer. As the future unfolds, we will need to review, reflect and rethink. As I mentioned in the first chapter, we are engaged in a voyage of discovery, in which the path to follow is making itself known while we are on the journey itself and we may have to do complete U-turns along the way.

Teleological decision-making

This is the term used to point out that quite often in life, as in work, the end calls the beginning. This method of decision-making starts with the end of a project rather than the beginning. What we do is to envisage and picture the end. Having a vivid image of what we would like to achieve is beneficial. From this image we work out what we have to do to arrive at this desired goal. Therefore, what we are doing is to reverse the usual pattern of planning by starting with the outcome. For this type of decision-making to work, it is important to have a clear image or a clear picture of what we would like the end of the project to look like. Using both left and right brain methods is very useful. Therefore we might draw a picture of our desired goal or imagine what it would look like. Having done so, we work out the steps which will take us to this desired outcome.

Activity 3.5

See the visualisation exercise in the previous chapter. Draw a picture, or prepare a collage of:

– How you would like your project to be at the end of a given period.
– What are the steps you need to take to arrive at this desired outcome?

If we use teleological planning, we have to be aware that nothing about the future is certain. But paradoxically the goal seems to invite a beginning and this is what we are drawing on. The path from the start to the outcome may be sinuous and at times may not make any logical sense. We also have to be prepared for the unexpected. We can have our dreams and the best way of achieving our dreams is to reconcile the paradox of very much desiring an outcome as well as letting go of the need to have the result we yearn for. It means, therefore, doing our best to achieve our outcome by engaging in activities which, it is hoped, will lead to this desired result but at the same time realising that our survival does not depend on us achieving this specific outcome. This letting go, in the belief that as mere human beings we have no control over the outcomes in life and that sometimes we do not know what is really the best alternative for us, is crucial. When we are able to engage paradoxically in both the active doing as well as the passive acceptance we are much more likely to actually achieve our outcome. But the road there may be full of surprises – each of these surprises being laden with learning opportunities for us.

The Gestalt cycle of energy use

The Gestalt cycle is a holistic model of the normal healthy use of energy. Therefore it is applicable to anything which we undertake, from feeling thirsty and drinking a glass of water to quench our thirst, to guiding us in our strategies for a project. The word "Gestalt" is a German word which is almost impossible to translate accurately into English. The "whole" is a close translation but this does not capture the essence of the meaning of the word. Therefore the word "Gestalt" has been retained in discussions of the model.

The cycle arises from a state of nothingness and a state of emptiness, known as the void: an empty space between things and events. This void is an important phase and as we shall go on to see, it is full of creative potential if we permit ourselves to experience this stage. Out of this nothingness where there is no clear form, we pick up a sensation. In Gestalt, we talk of a figure emerging as the sensation becomes apparent. The theory points out to us that at any moment in time,

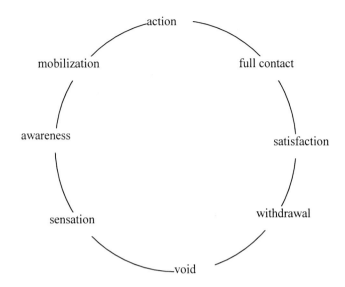

Figure 3.1. The Gestalt cycle of energy use.

something is the focus of our attention – the figure – while everything else constitutes the backcloth to that figure – the ground. When we experience a change of attention, whatever was ground becomes figure and the original figure becomes ground. At any split second, we can only focus on one figure while everything else becomes ground. As I am typing these words on a word processor, the words on the screen constitute the figure for me and everything else in my environment forms the ground. The telephone rings and the ringing of the telephone becomes the figure while what was figure – the words on the screen of my word processor – merges with the rest of the ground. Therefore, as soon as we notice something else, this becomes figure for us and the rest becomes ground.

To go back to the cycle itself, noticing a sensation is discerning a figure from a void. We become aware of the sensation: awareness, where we give meaning to the sensation. We move on to a stage of mobilisation which involves choice between different alternatives, followed by action and we engage in full contact with what we are doing. We then move into a state of satisfaction – where we reflect on the action. We can then withdraw from this particular activity or this particular focus and move back to another in-between space, another void, until another figure emerges as a sensation and so on. In the void itself, there is no clear and distinct figure and for this reason, many people find the nothingness of the void rather frightening.

To use a concrete example to illustrate the cycle, you may be in a void, not particularly focusing on anything and then you notice a feeling of dryness in your throat: a **sensation**. As you become aware of the sensation, you ponder on the meaning of the dry throat: maybe you are starting a sore throat or maybe you are just thirsty. You decide that you are thirsty: **awareness**. You choose which drink you will have: tea, coffee or a glass of water – **mobilisation**; you decide to drink water: **action** and you are aware of the water soothing your throat: **full contact**. Your throat feels better after taking the water: **satisfaction** and the figure of thirst disappears into the background: **withdrawal** and you enter another void. When we have completed a cycle, we can move back to another in-between space, i.e., another void and wait for the next sensation to emerge. This is the healthy and well-functioning cycle. In life we experience many major cycles and, of course, an endless number of mini-cycles.

For example, in a project each day is a cycle, in each of these days there are many smaller cycles, and there is a larger cycle. In a 3-year project we would have a large cycle of three years. This model can be applied to anything which we undertake and therefore can be utilized to help us in the decision-making process. The following example from a disability project illustrates the use of the cycle.

"When we first started our project, we had no idea of what we were going to do. Then I talked to some people and some of us went to the place of the project to find what was going on and what they wanted (void). The disabled people started to tell us of their needs (sensation). The disabled people had been telling the community their needs for some time but people in the community were not picking it up (awareness blocked at level of the community – project moving into awareness). My main role was to encourage the community to pick up the sensation and to become aware of what the sensation meant. In one

particular community, blind children were not going to school. That was the sensation/awareness we picked. Our role was to draw the attention of the community to that and to make them aware that blind children needed education. This was a major role for us and it took quite a long time. When they did finally become aware, then we could decide the alternatives open to us together (mobilisation); there were several open to us. They could be educated at home, they could go to a special school, or they could be integrated in the existing local school. In this case, after discussions we decided to integrate them into the school (action) and this took a long time to implement properly (full contact). We did a review of this part of the project and an evaluation of how this was working and we had quite a few celebrations (satisfaction). We could then leave this particular aspect of service to the disabled group which was by then fully integrated in the local community (withdrawal) and we moved on to another need which we were starting to pick up (beginning of another cycle)."

In the above example, there is a barrier to the smooth process of the cycle at the level of the community. An important role of this project is to release this blockage by getting the community to become aware of the sensation that blind children were not receiving any form of formal education.

Impediments to the smooth completion of the cycle

As noted above, sometimes there are impediments to completing the cycle. These serve a purpose, especially in the short term, where they may act as a means of protection. In the example of a feeling of thirst, if you happened to feel thirsty in the middle of an important interview for a job, you will note the sensation and become aware of its meaning. However, you would then probably decide not to quench your thirst immediately, as it would not be appropriate to seek a drink at that particular moment in time. But these impediments can also be dysfunctional, especially in the long term and when they are chronic ones. The unhelpful strategies we looked at earlier act as barriers to completing the cycle. These are particularly likely to be dysfunctional when they are the result of programmed behaviour by individuals and by organisations where people are repeating fixed patterns. In these situations, it would be beneficial to facilitate the completion of the cycle as in the example of the disability project, at the level of awareness which was dysfunctional for the blind children in that community who were missing out on schooling.

Activity 3.6

Identify cycles in your project and in your personal life. Can you recognise the many phases of the cycle?

Decision-making in the light of paradox

If we work with an "either… or…" way of thinking, we cannot deal with paradox. We become uncomfortable when we are faced with the existence of contradictions and we may resort to unhelpful stratagems to deal with the discomfort we experience. From a black-and-white, "either… or…" perspective, there is one correct answer and decision-making consists of finding out that one precise solution. When faced with paradox, which is normal in a complex uncertain world, to look for one single correct answer is not appropriate. We have to consider both sides of the contradictions. Some models help us deal with this predicament, but we have to bear in mind that we cannot ever totally resolve a paradox. There is not one accurate answer but many possible ones. As you will see, there are similarities and overlaps between the different models which are being suggested. Many of these models are quite ancient and have been used in other disciplines. In the face of complexity, these models become useful to the project leader.

The dialectical approach

The dialectical approach consists of considering both sides of the paradox and to confront them directly instead of wishing one of them away. It uses the model of thesis and antithesis leading to a synthesis. By that we mean that when we consider an issue, and we take full account of the opposite of what we consider, we will end with a totally new way of looking at the issue, which is the synthesis.

In a project this can be set up by having two groups of people with each group presenting the issue from one of its opposing sides. The process is similar to a debate except that in this case the outcome is not that of having one side winning over the other (an "either... or..." solution) but having a synthesis – a totally new outcome from the presentations – a "both... and..." approach.

The important aspect is not to run away from the opposing concerns, but to absorb both viewpoints and from this to discover the links between the opposites.

Synectics

This is a creative and innovative way of attempting to sort out a problem. What we do here is to look at a totally different context and sphere to find a solution. For example, if in a primary health care project you are not able to attract users, you might find out how the local popular singer attracts an audience, what you can learn from that situation and how you can apply what you learn to your project.

Creating opposition

The idea here is to create opposition on purpose. In decision-making, there is a strong tendency to take the first solution which fits our world view, the one which agrees with our premises, our assumptions, our deep seated beliefs and values. We are inclined to do our utmost to reject the ideas not in accordance with our own perspective. There is a strong propensity for human beings to stay within the framework which they know. As discussed in the previous chapter, there is a common tendency to work from within our known perspective. Therefore, we attempt to surmount this obstacle by making sure that we face the opposition. Someone acts as devil's advocate, taking on purpose the opposite view to the one which we take, thus forcing us to consider other solutions outside our own framework. Furthermore, when there is an agreement, we actually question this by seeking to find out what it is that we are not considering. This serves the purpose of making our assumptions explicit, so that we can review them and decide whether they still serve us well or whether we need to abandon them and change our premises and our assumptions.

The secret to this approach working is for us to concede as a starting point that the opposite perspective to ours may actually blend and merge with ours to give a better resolution to the problem which we are addressing.

The use of oxymorons

An oxymoron is a phrase which includes and links contradictory notions; for example, we may consider that the organisation should be a safe risk-taker, safe risk-taking being an oxymoron. Having stated the oxymoron, we consider the intrinsic, positive and negative characteristics of each of these two components.

So, in this example we need to look at the positive and the negative elements of a safe organisation, and then consider the positive and the negative components of the organisation which takes risks. From this discussion and this confrontation we can then decide how the organisation could be a safe risk-taker.

Another way of using oxymorons is to state a problem as an oxymoron and consider the negative and the positive in this image. Then, think of an ideal oxymoron for the problem and what would be the ideal. Consider your present situation in relation to the ideal and assess how well you are doing. Then look at the steps which you can take to bring you closer to the ideal oxymoron.

Polarity management

This is useful when there are two or more solutions, one of which we want to adopt while rejecting the others.

In this model we start by looking at the positives of the solution we prefer, and then we consider the negative aspects of the solution which we do not endorse. Having done these two steps, we find the negative aspects of the answer which we favour and we end by looking at the positive features of the solution which we do not desire. From this, we attempt a synthesis and a fusion of all the features which we have confronted.

Activity 3.7

Use any models proposed in the above section and work out how to reconcile the opposites and how to deal with the paradoxes in your project.

Creative methods for generating ideas

Brainstorming

A much-employed, although often misused technique, brainstorming is important in generating ideas. The aim is to have as many possible solutions, propositions and suggestions as possible. To work well, we need to aim for wild, illogical ideas. The reason that it is much misused is that too often judgment interferes with the production of ideas. It is crucial to suspend all judgment while brainstorming. Judgment is a later stage when we consider the feasibility of our ideas.

Analogy

With analogy we can look at a past situation and compare it to a present one. We find the patterns in both instances and use these to guide us. What we need to remember is that a new situation also has elements of the unknown and the uncertain about it. But we can be guided by the patterns we identify.

Another way of using analogy is to compare a present project with another context; this maybe another project or a very different organisation. Again we use the comparison to learn from the patterns we discover.

Activity 3.8

– What can you learn from a bank which can help you in improving your project?

– **Think about the negatives and the positives and what lessons you can deduce which would be useful to your project.**

Patterns in chaos: order in the midst of disorder

As we discussed earlier, chaos in the scientific sense of the word is not utter disorder; there are both order and disorder, known and unknown. There are patterns in work organisations and we use these to guide us in taking our decisions. A useful model is to think of a project or an organisation in terms of inputs, transformation and outputs.

In a project, we have desired outputs, i.e., what we set ourselves to achieve. We require inputs to the project. These include staff, resources such as money and equipment, as well as other particulars, for example, training. The transformation refers to the processes in which we need to engage to achieve our outputs. There are usually many alternatives we can consider when thinking through the processes and the activities we decide to carry out. Too often in projects, people merely reproduce the past and work within set patterns instead of thinking through new and creative ways of achieving the desired outputs. Some of these activities are key processes, vital to the organisation. We have to pay particular attention to these essential processes. It is also important to identify the variances, the discrepancies and what goes wrong in the performance of these consequential activities. An effective project closely monitors these processes and maintains quality by quickly correcting problems as they arise.

Identifying the primary task

The primary task of a project or an organisation can be defined in terms of what it has to do to survive and in terms of the difference it makes to the environment. A common problem in many projects is that there is no agreement about the primary task or that this is only vaguely defined. It is very useful to be clear about the primary task. We can use the above framework of input, transformation and output to help us in defining our primary task. For projects concerned with health and community services, the process involves people, i.e., people enter our system in one form and we would like them to leave in an altered state. As an illustration, in a community disability project, the input may be disabled children who do not have access to formal education and our desired output may be to have them fully integrated into schools. Making this kind of statement helps us in deciding the processes which are likely to lead to our desired output, so we have to ask ourselves what activities we need to engage in to achieve this outcome. Additionally, we have to consider the resources which we require to carry out these activities.

In the light of uncertainty and complexity, we have to note that there is a danger of using frameworks, as described in the above model, in a simplistic manner. We have to remember that there is much complexity in work organisations. For example, in a large project or organisation, there will be several sections, departments and subsystems with their own primary tasks which may be in conflict with those of other groups in the wider system. We also have to be aware that we need to change as we go along, responding to what is happening around us in the context of uncertainty. The model can guide us along the way while we remain sensitive to what needs to change. We do so, as stated earlier, by closely monitoring what is happening and feeding back the result of this monitoring activity into the system, thus setting up an iterative process – the process being changed along the way and the decisions and desired outputs being constantly reviewed.

Being aware of our interconnectedness

The manager or project leader has to take a broad view, noting the various ways in which our projects are connected to other sections of the wider organisation as well as to the external environment. This consists of ensuring the flow of information between her unit, the rest of the organisation and the environmental context and acting according to what occurs. For example, in a multi-disciplinary team of professionals, the various sub-units need to cooperate. Furthermore, a project manager has to be aware of what is happening in a wider sphere, considering important other stakeholders such as users of the project's services, external funders, international organisations and governments.

The manager's role is that of being clear about the task, ensuring that there are sufficient resources, verifying how the task relates to the wider organisation and to the external environment and of evaluating how well the project is doing in carrying out its task. Another important function is that of overseeing that the task is still relevant to the changing requirements of the wider organisation and of the wider environment. To be effective demands an awareness of the flux of uncertainty and of the complexities of the issues which are being addressed.

Project design

The following is a useful framework to guide us in our decision-making, by providing some guidelines as to what we have to consider. Again, this is not a rigid outline to be rigorously heeded; rather these are broad areas which need to be considered – the order, the patterns among the disorder and the chaos of complexity.

1. What is the primary task of the project, i.e., what difference does it make, what would not happen if the project did not exist? What does the project have to undertake to survive and thrive?
2. What are the inputs (people, resources, etc.)? Who can provide the inputs? Are people over- or under-utilised?
3. Who needs the outputs, who can use the outputs? Who are the clients of the project? How realistic are the desired outputs in view of the inputs available?
4. What transformation does the project need to engage in? What are the activities which the project has to undertake to change inputs into outputs? How creative and innovative is the project in transforming inputs into outputs? How does it deal with uncertainty and complexity?
5. How is quality controlled? What variances – that is deviations from what is proposed – occur during the transformation? How are these variances controlled? How quickly are variances recognised and

resolved? How good are the strategies for dealing with the deviation?

6. How does the project know whether it is successful in carrying out its task, i.e., what are the performance criteria? How is the project monitored? Is systematic evaluation carried out at regular intervals? Does the project use both quantitative and qualitative indicators to assess its progress?

7. What are the future options for the project/organisation? Can and should the project/organisation change its task or its area of work? How responsive is it to change in the external environment?

8. How complex and variable is the task? Is the appropriate mode of decision-making used for different activities?

It is also valuable to consider the various subsystems in a project, by carrying out an analysis of each subsystem and considering the implications for the wider project/organisation as well as the interconnectedness between the various subsystems.

1. Analysis of the user system

Who are our users? What do we need to do for them? How do we ensure that we listen to them and take note of what they say in the decisions we take? How do we monitor quality of service to users in terms of both the technical and relational components of the service we offer? Do we have to train our users on how to use our services?

2. Analysis of the social system of the project

What kind of staff do we require? How should we select them? What training do they need? How do we ensure the continuous development of staff?

Which activities are best carried out by individuals and which ones by teams of people? Do we engage in teambuilding? How do we encourage people to work in teams when this is required? Are there sufficient opportunities for informal social interaction? Do we encourage or hinder the workings of spontaneous self-organising groups? How do we as project leaders participate in the self-organising processes of the organisation?

3. Analysis of the technical system

What technical/professional expertise do we require? How do we ensure that this is adequate and that it meets the needs of our users? What opportunities are there for the continuous education and training of technical and professional staff? How do we encourage people to keep up-to-date with current developments in their fields of work? What equipment do we require?

4. Analysis of the workflow

What are the main operational stages of transforming inputs into outputs? What criteria do we have to measure how well we perform the various activities? How do we ensure that the workflow is functioning effectively?

5. Analysis of the support system

What support system do we have for staff? Do we have adequate support/ maintenance for the technical system and for the equipment we require? Do we have adequate information systems?

6. Analysis of the wider organisation and environment

How does our project fit into the wider organisation? How good is the information flow between our project and the rest of the organisation? How do we ensure adequate information flow between our project and the operational environment, including changes happening at the international as well as local and national levels? How do we ensure that our primary task responds to the needs and requirements of the wider operational environment?

7. Propositions for change

As we consider all the elements of a project including the fluctuating operational environment, we take decisions about what has to change. This includes considering whether we have to reframe and change the primary task itself as well as the processes in which we engage. Do we need to review the paradigms we use, the beliefs, the values and the assumptions which guide our work and our decision-making?

Realistic objectives – no utopia

When we take action in a project, it is crucial that our objectives should be feasible and realistic given the resources we have. Too often in projects the objectives are utopian. People become disillusioned and frustrated. They are unable to reach the desired goals as no human being can achieve utopian dreams. They have set themselves up to fail. This appears to be a common phenomenon amongst many projects in low- and middle-income countries. If we set realistic objectives and we achieve them, we feel successful, and success breeds success.

Decision-making in complexity: the continuous development of aspirations

To summarise, as the future is always uncertain, all long-term plans are problematic, but paradoxically we can and need to have our dreams. Therefore, we do formulate these aspirations, accepting, however, that we cannot possibly know in advance what will actually happen. Consequently, it means that we have to be very flexible and be ceaselessly prepared to change. As it is easier to speculate about the short-term future, we earnestly engage in short-term planning. To help us in deciding what we need to change, we constantly monitor our activities and our processes, taking note all the time of what is happening in the wider context. We monitor systematically at regular intervals as well as incessantly in an informal manner using all our senses. We constantly feed back the findings of this monitoring activity into the system, which thus becomes an iterative process. We are guided by the patterns which we can identify in projects and we use these patterns to raise important issues. We become aware that the best we can find in an imperfect world are solutions for to-day and that we may have to re-think in the future. We engage in the creative process, drawing on our intuition to counsel and direct us, taking into account the erratic and unpredictable manner of creativity. We test out the feasibility of our imaginative, original and inventive ideas by trial and error. Therefore, decision-making in complexity is not about having rigid and fixed objectives. But it is concerned with constantly generating strategies which, it is hoped, will lead to the achievement of our dreams and our aspirations. Very importantly, this involves being prepared to change both processes and outcomes along the way as the future unfolds.

Using left and right brain hemispheres

As we saw in the previous chapter, we need to use both left and right brain hemispheres for the process of decision-making. As we considered earlier, there are situations when the linear, rational model is the method of choice. There are circumstances where we know what to do, we can plan what we need to do and follow our plan. But as we have also seen, there are times when this is not so and we require other methods. Therefore, we have to engage in left and right brain thinking and move from one to the other as is appropriate. When we implement our ideas we have to constantly monitor what we are doing so that we can re-think and start again. We learn along the way and act according to what we learn. Most decisions involve taking a step into the unknown and the experience of the past may guide us but may also not be relevant. The unforeseen results of a decision sometimes prove to be more important than anticipated consequences. Parker and Stacey (1994) warn us that we take decisions in the here and now on the basis of data which were collected in the past and we hope to have results from this process for the future, therefore people are often acting on out-of-date information on the evidence of uncertain forecasts.

Therefore, it is crucial to learn and unlearn because decision-making in complexity becomes a process of discovery where the "truth" and the "correct" way keep changing. We have to learn to accept not knowing and to engage in a discovery process. As many writers on the topic have pointed out, today's solutions to yesterday's problems turn out to become to-morrow's nightmares. The best which we can achieve in a chaotic world, therefore, is to find the best possible resolution of an issue which will work for us today and is useful to us in the present.

Strategies therefore emerge and they do so from the many interactions which people have in the organisation. It is these interactions and these relationships which make up the organisation. We take decisions on the paradoxical notion that we cannot control the future but knowing that our aspirations will influence that future. As the future is revealed, we may have to re-think, re-formulate and change.

The following chapter considers important skills to help us along the way.

References and further reading

Parker D. and Stacey R. (1994) *Chaos, Management and Economics – The Implications of Non-Linear Thinking*, Hobart Paper 125, Institute of Economic Affairs, London.

Stacey R. (1993) *Strategic Management and Organisational Dynamics*, Pitman, London.

Chapter 4   Valuable perspectives to help us deal with complexity

The issue

In a complex world, we require certain personal skills, attitudes, beliefs and behaviours to enable us not only to survive but also to thrive. The implications of a complexity perspective as discussed in the preceding chapters call for distinctive attributes, abilities and competence. This means that to be successful project leaders and managers, we have to cultivate certain attitudes and ways of dealing with the world. A crucial step is to acquire and develop useful skills and perspectives. In an uncertain world, we cannot plan for what happens to us but we can be prepared so that we can handle what comes our way.

The construction of reality

Sociologists have pointed out how all reality is socially constructed. What is considered to be valid depends on historical, cultural, political and economic factors and changes from society to society and in the same society throughout time. At the individual level, we also construct our own reality. We do so by the way in which we see the world according to our beliefs, views, perspectives and values. We tend to screen out what does not concur with our own opinions and convictions. This process affects our projects, how we relate to people in the workplace and how we choose from the many alternatives open to us when we take decisions. Therefore, the paradigm within which we operate affects our work.

Valuable perspectives and outlook

To be proficient and masterful in dealing with complexity, some perspectives, attitudes and ways of looking at the world appear to be valuable.

The "both… and…" view of the world

Giving up black-and-white thinking is significant if we want to thrive in chaotic situations. In some instances, there are clear "either… or…" answers. We do have clear answers when we are dealing with relatively simple circumstances and with high levels of certainty. But much of what we undertake in managerial work and in project work is complex and occurs in contexts of uncertainty. In these situations, it is important to adopt the "both… and…" view of the world because as we have discussed previously we are dealing with paradox. We accept that opposites and contradictions occur simultaneously and that life and work consist of different shades of grey and cannot be resolved by an "either… or…" style of envisioning the world. We accept that contradictions, ambiguities and incongruities reign in the sphere of work. The most important outcome of espousing this way of thinking is that we stop looking for simple answers to the issues which we have to face, and we give up searching for prescriptions. These do not exist. If they did, the great leaders of the world would simply follow them. No one has a set of prescriptions for how to live and how to work. We can only have guidelines and principles: the patterns of chaos. But what we do with these patterns and how we use them will often change.

Activity 4.1

Consider the last time you were puzzled by something at work which was complex and uncertain.

– What was the issue?
– How did you deal with it? Were you looking for the single, correct answer?
– Were you aware of any paradox?
– What were the contradictions which were inherent in the issue?
– How did you personally feel about having to face contradictions?

In your own personal life, how do you react when you encounter paradox? How comfortable are you with being told that quite often there are no clear answers?

Multiple perspectives

In the same way that one person can be a father
to you and a son to someone else, an uncle
to another, and a nephew to yet another,
so what you are looking for
has many names, and one existence.

Don't search for one of the names.
Move beyond any attachment to names!
Every war, and every conflict between human beings,
has happened because of this disagreement
about <u>names</u>. It's such an unnecessary foolishness,
because just beyond the arguing,
there's a long table of companionship, set,
and waiting for us to sit down.

Rumi (1991) *One-handed Basket Weaving – Poems on the Theme of Work*, Versions by Coleman Barks, Maypop, Athens, Georgia, pp. 57–58

Another useful viewpoint is to be aware that, as there is so much variety among human beings, there are inevitably multiple perspectives when we look at any human systems. How funders, politicians, the local community and professionals look at a primary health care project or a disability project will be different. There are varying viewpoints and each one of them is valid in its own right. If we want to manage well, we allow these multiple perspectives to flourish and we do not silence those with whom we do not agree.

We can be in total dissent from someone else's viewpoint and still at a deep level respect that person and be grateful to him or her for forcing us to consider a different perspective. It is in the dialogue between these discords that we find new and innovative ways forward. If we all agree, we are in a state of ossification and over-stability and this is not good for us personally and for our projects. Dissent and conflict are to be encouraged and the existence of multiple perspectives is a cause for celebration. There will always be different realities. As we said earlier, we create our social realities. We interpret the world according to a pair of specific lenses which we wear. These lenses are the product of our upbringing, our environment, the cultures in which we operate and our own personalities. They are helpful in that they help us make sense of the world. But they can also be very obstructive as they filter what is in front of us. Our preconceived notions may impede us in our relationships with others in the here and now and may be a hindrance to fully engaging with situations we meet.

Activity 4.2

Think about your own project.

- **Who are the different stakeholders? How many groups of users do you have?**
- **What are the perspectives of these different groups of people about good service?**
- **How can you take these different outlooks into account in your work?**
- **What are the difficulties created by multiple perspectives in a project?**
- **What are the advantages of multiple perspectives to you, to your project, to your organisation and to the society in which you live?**
- **How can you encourage people to join you at "the long table of companionship" in spite of the different viewpoints?**

The normality of "mistakes"

In a chaotic world, we cannot avoid making mistakes. When the future is uncertain and issues are complex, we can only hope that the path we have chosen is the right one. But we cannot know whether this will be so in advance. No one can tell us that. Consequently, whatever we undertake is sometimes liable to not work. We cannot abstain from errors. What is crucial is that we reframe how we look at so-called mistakes. Mistakes are opportunities for learning. Many project leaders in low- and middle-income countries report that they work in circumstances where mistakes are not allowed. This is an untenable situation because, however efficient and capable we are as managers, at times we will generate errors. We cannot avoid doing so. Therefore we require an organisational culture which permits mistakes and does not punish people for the errors which are inevitable. Even if we cannot change the whole organisational climate, we can alter the culture for those who work for us. Within the power we have, we can attempt to convince our superiors that errors are sometime unavoidable. Furthermore, we have to point out to them that so-called mistakes are golden opportunities for us to learn something which may be worthwhile. As with differences of opinion, mistakes are a cause for celebration, the crucial question being what it is that we can learn from what has happened.

Activity 4.3

Is the organisational culture in your organisation supportive of people who make mistakes? What is it that you can do to demonstrate to colleagues and managers that some mistakes are inevitable and are good opportunities for learning?

The importance of shifting outside our habitual perspectives

As mentioned earlier, we tend to see the world from a customary outlook. Before reading on you might like to attempt the following activity.

Activity 4.4

Join the dots with four straight lines without lifting your pen/pencil from the paper:

O   O   O

O   O   O

O   O   O

This puzzle is one which most people are unable to do when confronted with it for the first time (see the end of the chapter for the solution).

As can be seen from the answer, the difficulty with solving this problem is that most people attempt to do so from within the framework of the nine dots. We have not been instructed that we cannot go outside the frame. Yet, most of us, when first given this puzzle, remain within the shape of the square. As the answer shows, to be able to solve it we have to go outside the frame and then it becomes fairly easy to resolve.

This little exercise illustrates a major point in that to deal creatively with work (and life) situations, we have to consciously venture outside our familiar perspectives. When we have done so, the former viewpoint will have radically changed and we will be seeing a different and often more useful picture.

Activity 4.5

Make a habit of believing impossible things – for a whole week, change your views about something on a daily basis.

Revelling in change as an important skill

As many writers are pointing out, in a chaotic and complex world, the only certainty is change itself. To welcome change into our lives and in our outlook is critical. Yet, most of us fear change and do our utmost to remain with what we have always known. This apprehension of change moves us either into a state of ossification where we hang on to our perspectives and seek stability or into a state of disintegration where we collapse. To go back to what was discussed in chapter one, it is useful to stay in the chaotic edge where we become creative in the face of change. To behave as if everything is static in a project is a sure recipe for disaster. Therefore an awareness of continuing change is important for our work. Part of our personal development as project leaders and managers is to learn to welcome change into our lives so that we can be flexible and adaptable. To do so includes the practice of change in our daily living. The following activity allows us to be prepared for and confident with change and is one which many prominent authors on the subject suggest that we should exercise on a regular basis.

Activity 4.6

On a weekly (or even daily) basis, practice changing what you normally do, e.g., if for breakfast you usually have tea, have another drink instead; get out of bed on the opposite side to the one you normally choose; wear different clothes to work, etc.

The above activity may appear to be insignificant, but it is in effect a very important one. It prepares us for dealing with change so that we are better equipped when it is crucial for us to do so.

As circumstances around us alter, we allow ourselves to change our minds about what we used to cherish and to keep on reserving the right to keep revising our perspectives. In other words, we do not remain static in our beliefs, attitudes and perspectives but grant ourselves the permission to re-think as the future unfolds.

Embracing paradox

The normal nature of paradox in the workplace has been discussed previously. However, at the individual level, many people are troubled by being told that in many circumstances there are no clear answers to our issues. These people want the security which direct answers provide. They hope that they will be given prescriptions on how to manage their projects. They are distressed to hear that we do not have blueprints which we can hand out to project leaders.

To deal effectively with the workplace, we have to accept that in many situations there are no direct solutions. There are certain things about which we are sure and in these cases, we do have straightforward answers. But in many circumstances this is not so and we are faced with contradictions, inconsistencies and ambiguities. Acceptance that this is the case is critical. Also important is the acknowledgement that there are multiple solutions. Furthermore, we often do not know in advance whether our choice of solution will work or not. Only time will tell us if this is so. Embracing paradox is therefore crucial; the aim is to be comfortable with questions which remain unanswered. It is the raising of the questions themselves which is fruitful – for many important things in life we have no clear answers but living the questions is highly fruitful.

Activity 4.7

Reflect on how you personally deal with paradox, ambiguities and contradictions.

- **What emotions and feelings do you experience when faced with the above?**
- **What is your behaviour in these circumstances?**
- **Do you believe that there must be a single answer when confronted by paradox?**
- **What effect does reading this paragraph have on you?**
- **What can you do to be more comfortable with paradox?**

Acceptance and confrontation: combining the "feminine" and the "masculine" principles

We meet another paradox in that we have to combine the passive, more "feminine" principle of acceptance with the active "masculine" attribute of confrontation to be a successful project leader. I am using these terms here not to denote the female and male genders but in the sense given by the Chinese principle of yin and yang. We have to accept the existence of contradictions and at the same time we have to be active in considering the merits of these contradictions. We are, therefore, presented with another paradox in that effective management is this combination of acceptance – a passive stance – and confrontation and challenge – an active position.

Recognition of constant flux in life and in projects

For those of you who live in or who have travelled to the colder parts of the world, the four seasons represent a good model for the constant cyclical change which we often meet at work and in our private lives. We need the darkness and the coldness of Winter (death) to bring forth the growth and the newness of Spring (birth) which then develops into the glory of Summer (life), followed by the transition phase of Autumn which is decline into yet another Winter. This cyclical model, which is found in many stories, myths and religions, offers us a symbol for the chaotic nature of work and of life. This cycle begins with death followed by a rebirth and life to move once again to a state of death. We have therefore a constant movement, with death being the beginning of a new cycle. By this we mean that destruction precedes the emergence of something new. We shall re-visit this later on when we look at change. For the moment, we need to recognise the constant cyclical movement. There is no finite ending but instead a state of perpetual flux. For example, we note that circumstances may not be auspicious, that they get worse and they reach such a level that they can only get better – which they eventually do – and consequently they become so favourable that they can only start to get unfavourable again. It is the realisation that when we are baffled and puzzled and are not moving on, that this phase will eventually pass, and, of course, the reverse being that when we are doing extremely well and feel that we have reached the top, that this also will pass! The acceptance of this normal cycle and of this continuous rise and fall, as with the ebbing and waning of a tide, is crucial to project leaders. This leads to the perpetual learning process which we have to adopt if we want to be effective. A crucial skill for project leaders and managers in the midst of uncertainty and complexity is the ability to tolerate the difficulties and the bad times which we all experience.

Activity 4.8

Identify the cyclical patterns which you observe in your project and your work organisation.
Next, identify the cycles in your personal life.

– **How aware are you of those cycles?**
– **How do you deal with them, especially when things are not going so well for you?**

"Riding the waves"

Morgan (1988) talks about how managers and organisations have to deal with wave after wave of changes and that this is now a crucial aspect of work organisations and for him "riding the waves" is an apt metaphor for facing the complexity and continuous change in organisations.

Some of you will be familiar with the sport of surfing which consists of riding on the crests of the waves of the sea. To do so requires superb skills. The surfer lets go of control while controlling. This paradox is a useful metaphor for work organisations. Project leaders have to face very many waves. The adept manager knows how to ride the waves, i.e., how to confront as well as when to let go of control. Riding the waves involves taking advantage of the flow when it is in our favour and retreating and letting go when it is not. As discussed earlier, this demands both "feminine" acceptance and "masculine" confrontation.

"How to fall down and get up again"

Clarkson (1995), in reviewing the skills we need for a complex world (see further reading), talks of the need for being able to fall down and get up again; being able to yield and concede that one has met a setback and re-start.

Sometimes the waves are much too strong for us and we cannot avoid falling down, even the best skilled surfer does fall from her/his surf board. What is involved here is the recognition that we cannot, at times, escape from falling down and making mistakes. It entails the acknowledgement that mistakes are learning points and are not a sign of deficiency and inadequacy. Failure consists of falling down and not getting up again. Competent managers fall down but they do get up and are prepared to start this cyclical process over and over again.

Activity 4.9

– What happens when you "fall down" in the course of carrying out your work?
– What are the emotions which you experience, what is your

behaviour?
– What do you do to "get up" again?
– What /who helps you in getting up?
– If you have difficulties in "getting up" again, identify what leads to your not doing so.
– What can you do to change?

Working with energy

As we keep noting, cyclical models are helpful in that they follow the natural course of events and the spontaneous sequence of change we meet in the natural world. In the chapter on decision-making, we described the Gestalt model as a useful cyclical model which managers can use in projects. We also need to consciously work with energy patterns. Levels of energy change as we go through a cycle. When we engage in an activity, the typical flow of energy gradually increases until it reaches a peak before it starts to wane again. In work organisations, one often finds that people do not make use of this natural pattern, instead they strive to force the flow of energy, attempting to get others involved in important matters when energy is very low and, conversely, not making use of high levels of energy. It also seems that the ideal time period for the use of energy is a 90-minute cycle. We can make use of this very favourably in the workplace. For example, meetings can be held to last 90 minutes and no more, or when we need to write a report we can schedule a 90-minute slot of undisturbed time. We require a period of rest when we exceed that time; therefore to have adequate breaks is a very effective way of working. When energy is much too low, it may be wiser to postpone an activity and permit people to rest or reflect on their work. The effective manager also knows how to stimulate energy in workers by inspiration and enthusiasm.

Regarding energy, not only should there be peaks of activity, but we also need quieter, reflective time when we move into non-action as is well demonstrated by the Gestalt cycle of energy. When we follow the flow of energy, carrying out a task becomes effortless, while struggling against the flow means that we are also struggling in our efforts.

Activity 4.10

What are the signs of low levels of energy in your work organisation, and what are the signs of high levels of energy?

– How can you capitalize on high levels of energy?
– What can you do when energy levels are running low?

Learning preceded by unlearning

You've heard descriptions
of the ocean of non-existence.

Try, continually, to give yourself
into that ocean. Every workshop
has its foundations set
on that emptiness.

The Master of all masters
works with nothing.

The more nothing comes into your work,
the more God is there.

Rumi (1991) *One-handed Basket Weaving – Poems on the Theme of Work*, Versions by Coleman Barks, Maypop, Athens, Georgia, pp. 122

We have several times mentioned the importance of learning. But to learn at a profound rather than a superficial level means that we have first to unlearn (Clarkson, 1995). Unlearning involves de-struction of what we already know and most of us are very frightened by any type of destruction. We do not learn if we hold on to our previous beliefs, assumptions and knowledge. We have to be prepared to accept that what we have espoused sincerely may no longer be adequate. Reflecting on what goes on in the world and in the workplace shows that the solutions to yesterday's issues often turn out to be the problems of the future. It seems that, to a large extent, we cannot escape this occurring, as it is so difficult for us to anticipate what will happen in the future. Therefore it is important to be continuously prepared to unlearn so that we can find new ways forward.

Giving up what is dear to us is painful, and most of us, in protecting ourselves from that pain, choose to stay with obsolete models which no longer work for us. If we go back to the nine-dot activity, we find that each time we learn something new, we are once again in the "prison" of the nine dots. We have re-constructed new perspectives and new lenses for looking at the world and, of course, they serve us in the present. Yet, sooner or later, these also will become inadequate. Therefore when that stage is reached we have to step outside the frame again. We have to unlearn and obtain yet another pair of lenses which may sometimes in the future become inadequate and so on. If we go back to the section on cyclical processes we find that each unlearning is a "death". This death is painful and sorrowful for us, although sometimes we also paradoxically feel excited and elated at the same time. These are the satisfaction and the withdrawal stages of the Gestalt cycle. We have to withdraw from what we already know and face the void, the nothingness and the emptiness once again so that a new figure, a new form and a new shape will emerge. This happens when we are ready to face the "death"; when we are prepared to experience the distress, the grief and the sadness of giving up the old. We have to experience dying so that re-birth can take place.

Project leaders have to get rid of their old mindsets which are no longer useful so that they can embrace new ones. The pain of unlearning cannot be avoided. Pain is part and parcel of life and we have to accept this. But there is also the excitement of the new. Therefore we have to deal with the de-struction which precedes re-construction. In our work, we have to constantly work from a place of "nothingness" as if we do not know anything at all, for it is from that emptiness that we re-discover and re-construct.

Taking part in the action: being involved

As we are all interrelated in this world, we have to be actively engaged. We cannot not take part. By remaining passive, we do take part. Therefore, we have to develop an awareness of what we choose to do and what we choose not to do. Both our actions and our non-actions have a consequence. We have to take responsibility for these. Clarkson (1996) draws our attention to the phenomenon of by-standing (see further reading). We are by-standers when we remain passive and simply watch when in effect we can act and help; we are able to assist but we refrain from acting. By-standing is very disempowering.

Adaptability and flexibility: the importance of listening

What all this demands from us is a high level of adaptability and flexibility. We have to be prepared for whatever comes our way instead of being rigid. Part of this means being an active listener and really hearing what is being said to us – verbally and non-verbally. Most of us do not really listen, as we are busy rehearsing what we are going to say next – instead of taking on the whole message which another is trying to communicate to us. Listening can be a risky activity as we can be changed in the process. We listen with the person when we take note of what is being said and we listen for the person when we notice what is not being said but what is being conveyed during the interaction. Listening for the unspoken both verbally and non-verbally is a crucial skill for managers. This involves being in touch with people and having meaningful relationships with those around us.

Interconnectedness – "agape" in the workplace

We cannot operate in isolation. In this world, we are all interconnected. Relationships matter very much, for it is through relationships that we make our most meaningful contributions to the workplace and to the universe and it is through the interactions and relationships we make and through our networks that strategies emerge. In our work relationships, we are not asked to like the people with whom we deal at an emotional level. It does mean that we have to "love" them. In English, the word love is used indiscriminately to refer to different types of love. The Greek work "agape", which is translated in English by the word love, is what I have in mind here. Agape means respecting the dignity of the other, seeing the divine in other people, valuing the soul of those around us. Although we may not feel that we like these people, we show consideration and reverence for them as human beings.

Being aware of our interconnectedness also involves appreciating the effect we have on others and taking responsibility for this. What we choose to do or what we choose not to do has a consequence for others in the short and long term. Therefore, we need to be conscious of this as we go about our daily work. It is almost inevitable that we should experience some relationship difficulties at work. Dealing with people is difficult and complex and to make mistakes in relationships is unavoidable. But each person we come across has a lesson or a learning point for us. People do not cross our paths by chance. When we have difficulties, we have to ask ourselves what are the learning points in that relationship. What is known as the "entanglement theory" points out to us that at a deep level we are influenced by and remain connected to the individuals we have met for the rest of our lives. When we are in a relationship with people, at a very profound level we are in a state of continuous change.

Working with groups

It is crucial that project leaders and managers learn how to work with groups. We cannot avoid groups, as a work organisation is by definition a group. Here a group is defined as people coming together and having a common task. It is at the level of the group that most things are identified, defined and given a value. The notion of individuality is itself problematic as no one is "an island"; whether we are conscious of it or not, we are affected by groups around us. Complexity shows how we self-organise spontaneously and this involves, of course, operating at the group level. Groups can self-organise in the most wonderful and creative ways, using the synergy of the group to produce extraordinary work. Or they can self-organise in destructive, fixed and unhelpful patterns. There is a tendency for groups to work with the past or to be concerned with the future and not work with the here and now. Wise project leaders encourage groups to work with the present – with what is important at this minute of this unique day. To become aware of the magical dimension of every second of each day is also vital. Working with the present, project leaders have to become attentive to what is emerging from the group, what is getting their attention right now and what is the figure for them. Good work is done when we note what is surfacing, when we become aware of the figure and work with that and not with what has been decided as an agenda, which may have no relevance for people at this moment in time. The secret of successfully managing people is to work with what gets their attention and not with what we think is important for them.

It is useful to become conscious of the dynamic process of groups, and how they change day by day.

Skills for dealing with the void

The void is that space or that emptiness which we face when we are letting go of an episode, an event, a situation or an encounter so that we may engage with another experience. It is that space in between spaces and the hiatus between completing a cycle and starting a new one. Many people experience the void as difficult. Often at this stage we have no clear figure to guide us and human beings are comforted by distinct shapes and patterns. When the figure is unclear, we have a tendency to become distressed. While many people feel troubled by being in a void, others find the experience exciting and exhilarating. For those who are distressed by being in this space, it is worth remembering that this is potentially very creative and if we learn to let go and trust that sooner or later we will know what to do, eventually a clear figure emerges and we can start a new cycle. The important thing in the void is to let go, i.e., letting go of the need to control, letting go of the need to always know and to understand, as well as trusting that our subconscious will guide us along the way. It is useful at this stage to simply stop working at a solution and to spend the time carrying out all the routine tasks which we need to undertake. Therefore this is a good time to sort out our mail, to work out a better administrative system, do any filing, clear out the clutter which we accumulate in our offices and so on. It is also a good time to improve our working relationships with others and engage in team-building activities. It is also important to ensure that we have plenty of relaxation. If we are able to stay in that space, however uncomfortable we feel at first, eventually we do receive the insight and we do reach the "aha" experience as our intuition and our right brain functions take over and tell us what we have to undertake. If we have the skills to deal with the vacuum of the void, it becomes a fruitful one. If we do not handle this space effectively, the void may turn out to be a futile one (Clarkson, 1992). Our aim as project leaders is to turn the abyss of the void into a fruitful venture.

Activity 4.11

Reflect on how you deal with the void. What emotions do you encounter? How effective are you in that space?

– **How good are you at letting go and waiting for a clear picture to emerge?**
– **Do you have sufficient trust and confidence in yourself?**
– **What can you do differently to make the experience a fruitful one?**

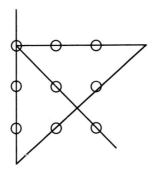

Figure 4.1. Solution to 9- dot puzzle (Activity 4.4).

References and further reading

Clarkson P. (1992) *Gestalt Counselling in Action*, Sage, London.

Clarkson P. (1993) *On Psychotherapy*, Whurr, London.

Clarkson P. (1995) *Change in Organisations*, Whurr, London.

Clarkson P. (1996) *The Bystander*, Routledge, London.

Morgan G. (1988) *Riding the Waves of Change – Developing Managerial Competencies for a Turbulent World*, Jossey Bass, San Francisco.

Rumi (1991) *One-handed Basket Weaving – Poems on the Theme of Work*, Versions by Coleman Barks, Maypop, Athens Georgia.

Chapter 5   Empowerment and self-development

The issue

Previous chapters have looked at what it means to deal with complexity and uncertainty in projects. Project leaders and managers require particular qualities, attitudes and frames of mind. Managers, their workers and the organisation have to engage in a continuous learning process: constantly unlearning and learning. To be able to undertake the challenges of a complex world and particularly to possess the competencies required, we need to ensure our own development. By engaging in personal development, we are able to realize our potential and we become empowered; a powerless and helpless project leader is of no use to an organisation. Management by definition means that we believe that we can influence what happens. The next chapter will discuss the important role which managers have in developing other people in the work organisation. To be able to incite and inspire others to learn we have to be engaged constantly in our own personal growth. The personal development of the project leader and manager is therefore important.

A chaotic model of development

In a world where linear models predominate, development is often viewed as a steady and usually vertical advancement with ever-increasing gains and progress. However, this model of development is not a useful one, because in reality any attempt to improve ourselves is often marked not only by progress and advancement but also by stagnation, backward steps and difficult and traumatic times. These times are useful to us and full of learning potential. The model which I suggest here is a chaotic one, where people not only value the periods in which they feel they are advancing, but also learn and gain from the periods of stagnation and of regression. Development is not a neat linear progression, but a cyclical process where at times there is no advancement and we have to unlearn and start all over again. These troublesome and perplexing moments are part and parcel of the process of development. We need to learn to accept them and to maximise the potential of these times. The void, the darkness and the not knowing form part of the developmental process and need to be appreciated. Phases of stagnation and even of regression can be fertile ground, even if emotionally it may be difficult to live through them. To be able to live and work healthily in a chaotic world, we need to be able not only to fully appreciate the good times but very importantly to tolerate and abide troublesome and perplexing periods.

Starting with oneself

Leaders concerned about development need to start with themselves. The following story is told about Mahatma Gandhi. A woman brought him her young son, asking him to advise the child to cease eating sweets which were damaging his teeth. To the surprise of the woman, Gandhi asked her to return with her son in two weeks time. The woman came back at the agreed time. Gandhi looked at the little boy and asked him to promise that he would stop eating so many sweets. The bewildered woman asked Gandhi why he had not done so when she first brought her son to see him, to which Gandhi replied: "Two weeks ago, I was myself eating sweets."

This little anecdote points out to us the importance of seeing to our own personal development and learning before we attempt to develop our workers and the organisation. Effective leaders lead by example. By engaging in our own continuous development, we are more likely to be influential in encouraging others around us to undertake their own development.

Doing and being

Professionals possess a "doing" part, i.e., that aspect of themselves which is concerned with performance, achievement and receiving recognition and with what gives them a position and a status in life. Professional development generally is concerned with "doing", providing us with the knowledge and skills necessary to further our competency in what we achieve. This is an important part to be cultivated for the enhancement of our work and is necessary for the technical aspect of our work. However, there is another side which is as important and this is our "being". This refers to the intimate, private part of ourselves, concerned with our essence and with how to become more fully who we really are, taking into account our own personal gifts and talents. Whenever we are able to combine this "doing" with our "being", the work we produce has a different feel, an underlying quality which is far superior to the outcome of our work when we operate only from "doing" (see Clarkson, 1995). Combining the "doing" and the "being" leads us to engage in "soul work".

In the workplace "doing" is emphasised. Productivity is generally what counts. This is, of course, important for our projects and we have to justify being paid by an organisation. But our work is not only about "doing", it is part and parcel of ourselves, so in a way some of our "being" is closely connected to our paid work. Although work organisations stress doing and it is fitting that they should do so, who we are has an impact on what we do and how we do it. Therefore developing the "being" side of ourselves will inevitably have an impact on the "doing". Personally, we also gain as our "doing" comes to reflect the essence of who we are.

Some organisations recognise this and ensure that their managers engage in their own personal development so that they can merge the "doing" and the "being" and as a result, are not only personally more satisfied about their work, but also enhance the quality of the work they produce. However, in most work organisations, the "doing" part is the one which is generally emphasised, as this is what leads directly to increased productivity with thought given to the technical aspect of the work and to professional development. To counteract the overemphasis on "doing", it is worthwhile to think about developing the "being" aspect of ourselves. We do so when we focus on who we are, when we aim to discover our talents and to develop them, and when we find out our calling in this world so that we may become the person we are meant to be. When we develop both our "doing" and our "being", we are able to carry out extraordinary work.

For many people in low- and middle-income countries, the development which is available and encouraged concerns the "doing" rather than the "being". Some of the reading at the end of this chapter will provide some suggestions for self-help in terms of our own personal development and a few ideas about how to do so are included in this chapter. When we engage in a life-long quest for our individual development, not only do we personally benefit, but our work organisation does so as well. Too many managers go through life focusing only on their professional development – the "doing" – and they ignore or fail to engage in personal development – the "being". By emphasising the "doing" we may be very effective and good at climbing promotional ladders, but for many this means that in spite of the external success, they keep on being dissatisfied with life at a deeper level. For some people, this leads to finding even more challenges for the "doing" aspect of themselves and even more ladders to climb with the hope that each promotion will bring the happiness which they seek but sometimes do not find.

Developing the "being" part of ourselves is not essential for achievement in the workplace. However, what it does bring to work is a different dimension and a deeper meaning; the quality of our work is generally greatly improved. It is therefore valuable for managers to cultivate the "being" aspect, to engage in their own personal development as well as seeking to improve their technical expertise through professional development. For a more profound experience in the workplace, we need the merging of the "being" and "doing".

The search for meaning

Having meaning in one's life is something important to human beings. Work is one of the ways in which we bring meaning to our existence. When we combine "being" with "doing" at work we discover our special purpose. Our motivation to work well is greatly enhanced. We experience intrinsic motivation where the wish to work well and to do the best we can is part of our nature and there is a strong urge to do so. In this way, our particular gifts and talents are fully used for our own personal benefit and to the advantage of the organisation for which we work. This becomes "soul work" and in this way we give so much more to the work organisation to which we belong. In so doing, we also contribute to humanity and to the universe – an important aspect of existing on this earth. To discover one's special talents, and then fully use them at work is a means of giving meaning to our lives. It is when we feel that we are fulfilling ourselves that we are best able to work well and are able to help others around us do the same.

Being, doing and complexity

As we saw in the previous chapters, working in conditions of uncertainty and complexity demands special skills. We can improve on these competencies in what we do, but developing these capacities fully involves changing ourselves at a deeper level; it involves our "being" and the merging of the two, forming a "Gestalt" or a whole, producing a holistic approach to our work.

Activity 5.1

Make a collage or a drawing of the path from the time you started work to the present time. Make another one about your dreams for your work from the present time to when you choose to retire.

- **What special talents do you personally possess?**
- **What are the things which you particularly enjoy? Are you able to use these in the workplace?**
- **What aspects of yourself can you use to enhance the quality of your work?**
- **What unique contributions can you make to the workplace, to your fellow workers and, by extension, to the universe?**

Dealing with our fears

As we have seen previously, faced with the turbulence of the world in which we work, individuals and organisations tend to retreat into unhelpful strategies instead of finding creative outcomes. Fear is a major stumbling block along the way to deal with complexity effectively. Consciously and unconsciously we become anxious from an unknown and unknowable future. Dealing with anxiety is a major task for project leaders and managers. As stated earlier, we cannot do for others what we cannot do for ourselves. Therefore in learning to deal with our own fears, our own anxiety is crucial. The best way of handling fear is to face it and not to pretend that it is not there. Paradoxically, when we do so, we become enabled to react; we are able to take the energy and use it productively and constructively. It is important to remember that inspiration and anxiety are closely linked to each other. Any complex learning situation inevitably involves a certain level of anxiety. But many people give in to their fears and become overwhelmed by negative feelings. Anxiety used constructively is a means of problem-solving. The emotion we experience encourages us to examine alternatives and find suitable solutions to a problem. We can change anxiety and fear into excitement as we take the step into the unknown future. Chronic and repetitive anxiety is very disempowering, although many people seem to gain a pay-off from perpetual worrying. The following exercise is useful when we find ourselves worrying constantly and unable to take decisions.

Activity 5.2

When you find yourself continuously worrying, first become aware of what you are doing – this state of awareness is an important first step. Second, find a means of relaxation: physical activity, meditation, relaxation, etc. Third, face the problem:

– Is the problem a real one, what is the nature of the problem?
– What is the worst possible scenario and what can you do to cope with this? What are the various alternatives open to you, what constructive steps can you take?

Trusting our own potential and being aware that human beings possess the capabilities to find their way through chaos and complexity is an important way of confronting fear.

This involves believing in oneself and having good self-esteem.

The importance of self-esteem

Our self-esteem reveals our measure of self-acceptance and how worthwhile we believe we are. It is a good indicator of our psychological well-being and is related to our own confidence in ourselves. Our level of self-esteem affects how we live, work and relate to others. It does fluctuate according to our interactions with others and with what is happening in our lives.

Managers with good enough self-esteem are secure in their abilities to take decisions, to solve problems, to give and receive feedback and are more likely to be sensitive to others. When we feel good about ourselves, it is easier for us to accept responsibility for our choices and our actions and we are less tempted to exercise power over others.

Unfortunately, we have all received many negative messages about ourselves from our past and from present situations which affect our self-esteem. These messages are likely to have affected how we perceive ourselves. Therefore, we need to counteract their damaging effect.

Activity 5.3

Make a list of twenty of your good qualities, talents and abilities.

- **For a whole week, add at least two more to this list on an everyday basis.**
- **Keep this list in a safe place and look at it whenever you are feeling dejected and experience low self-esteem.**

Positive thinking

Being recipients of negative points means that many of us have internalised these destructive messages and have come to believe the labels that have been conferred on us by others. We also give ourselves many negative criticisms, belittling ourselves, our achievements, our capabilities and our talents. To be effective managers, it is important to rectify this situation. Positive thinking is crucial if we want to survive and succeed in a chaotic and complex world. This involves avoiding looking at issues and at ourselves in a negative manner.

Activity 5.4

Make a habit of noticing your thoughts and of listening to the internal voice which you use to speak to yourself.
- **What sort of messages do you give yourself?**
- **Are they predominantly negative or positive or a mixture of the two?**
- **In what circumstances are you more likely to give yourself negative messages?**
- **How can you redress this? What positive messages can you give to yourself?**

Activity 5.5

Whenever you notice a negative thought, tell yourself to stop the negative thinking.
Re-formulate your thought into a constructive one or engage in some positive thinking: think of positive issues and replace your negative thoughts by these positive ones.

Affirmations

Affirmations are a powerful way of maintaining our self-esteem. The aim is to give yourself positive messages in order to validate yourself. We can affirm and value ourselves without being conceited and egoistic. To respect and value others, we have to respect and value ourselves first. Furthermore, to develop our potential, we have to remind ourselves of our positive points. Affirmations are also useful for us to achieve a particular goal. If our belief system gives us the permission to achieve that goal, it is much easier for us to do so in practice. For example, top achievers in the field of sports use affirmations to maximise the possibility of success. The aim is to regularly restate positive statements. Affirmations are very potent in diminishing the power of the many negative messages which have come our way over the years and which have affected our sense of self-worth. They also negate the many dis-empowering judgments we pass on ourselves. They are efficacious in helping us to regain and retain our self-esteem and they encourage a positive frame of mind. They are also helpful when we face difficult situations or when we are having to deal with people who negate our sense of self-worth and who devalue us.

Activity 5.6

Use affirmations regularly. You can use affirmations both for "being" and for "doing". There are some important guidelines in constructing your own affirmations. For these to be effective, use "I" statements in the present tense, employ positive phrases and be realistic. Examples of useful affirmations:

– I am a good enough project leader.
– I take creative decisions.
– I am a positive person.
– I see the positive in situations and in people.
– I know how to deal with difficult situations.
– I am a talented and sensitive manager.

The aim is to make your own affirmation according to your needs and the situations in which you find yourself.
Repeat the affirmations to yourself either quietly in your own mind or out loud if this is appropriate. In difficult times, it is useful to make affirmations, write them and place them around your office or your home to remind yourself of the messages.
Another powerful way of using them is to repeat them out loud while looking at yourself in a mirror – until the eyes in the mirror confirm that you really believe what you are saying.
It is important to use them regularly.

Affirmations may sound foolish and nonsensical but they really do make a difference. If you find yourself resistant to using them, remind yourself that successful people in the fields of entertainment, sports and business use them regularly, as well as developing a positive frame of mind; they would not do so if affirmations were not effective.

Living life fully

What makes us energetic and creative beings is the life force and the life energy which all human beings possess. It is what urges us to go on when we have "fallen down", it is what spurs us to use our talents and our potential and it is what makes us the people we are. Too often we do not use this amazing life force which is in all of us. We squander it and do not respond fully to life. The question for us is: to what extent are we using our life force? Are we really alive, half asleep or simply dragging a "corpse" when we are at work? Our life force is there for us in the face of chaos and complexity. It entreats us to fully take part in life and not wish that things were different for us. The positive and the negative aspects of chaos are life challenges and opportunities for us. We cannot afford to waste the marvellous potential, talent and ability within each one of us. To go back to an important point made earlier, to indulge in wishful thinking about how things could be, or how others will or ought to save us, will not be of any help to us. The question which we have to continually face is simply "what are we going to do"?

Work (and life) is stormy, turbulent and difficult and at the same time it is challenging, exciting and empowering.

Taking responsibility and knowing when we are not responsible

The contradiction of this subtitle involves the art of knowing when to take responsibility for our actions and what happens to us – as well as refusing to be held responsible when the impossible is being expected of us; this is what some authors have called the shame-game.

An important means of retaining and developing our personal power is that of taking responsibility. Earlier we have looked at the disempowering effect of engaging in blaming others. The essence of accepting responsibility is to find out what it is that we can do in any situation. To a large extent, we create the reality of what happens. How we choose to react to predicaments is entirely within our power. Even when we are unable to intervene actively and change a situation, we can use the experience as a learning point.

Empowered project leaders are those who take responsibility for what they can achieve and act on this responsibility. First, we need to be fully aware of what the situation entails and second, take responsibility for what we can do. Accepting responsibility means response-ability, i.e., we are able to respond to what is happening. Once again, combining "doing" and "being" leads to a more profound resolution. The more aware and conscious we become of who we are at a deep level, the freer we are in deciding what response to give to a situation.

However, the empowered project leader refuses to take on responsibility for impossible and utopian aims and objectives.

Sarah is a project leader with an international NGO. She is a hard and conscientious worker who strongly believes that her work is very worthwhile. However, she is highly stressed, not only from overwork but also because she feels that she is unable to meet the demands and the expectations of her managers and the funders. She feels guilty for being unable to achieve what they expect of her. The quantitative health indicators used by the project show no real improvement in health in spite of her efforts. This is a very disadvantaged area where poverty has increased dramatically in the last few years. Sarah believes that this is partly due to the policies of structural adjustment. She knows that poverty is the major cause of ill health and recognises that at best her project can only have a minimal effect. The action of governments is what is required. But she still believes that she should be able to meet the demands of producing hard indicators of health to show an improvement. She experiences strong feelings of shame when funders come to visit the project or when she reports back to head-quarters. She lives in fear that the project will be closed down. She knows that she contributes to the psychological well-being of the local women but this is difficult to demonstrate and there are no measures of quality and of "soft" outcomes in this project.

Here we have a situation where the project leader accepts feeling shame for what she cannot possibly achieve. No human being can meet unrealistic and utopian objectives, as we have discussed in the chapter on decision-making. In many situations we are not responsible for what happens. Either we are asked to achieve what cannot realistically be achieved or things are beyond our control. This latter point is made clear when we look at complexity where we have to accept the unpredictable, what is outside our control and also the absurdity of the world. There are many circumstances where we cannot even start to comprehend what is going on. The world is an absurd one where not everything is amenable to logical understanding. Moreover, as multi-causality is the norm in work organisations and there are very complex interrelationships between cause and effect, we cannot be held culpable for everything which happens. If others attempt to make us accountable for the unaccountable, or expect us to achieve utopian objectives when we are but mere mortals, then it is not our fault and not our responsibility. If project leaders and managers do not wish to feel dis-empowered, they have to be assertive enough to refuse to be ashamed of what they cannot humanly accomplish; they need to refuse blame and liability for what is outside their control and, at the same time, they have to act responsibly in terms of what they can realistically undertake.

The secret of empowerment: the perception of choice

In all circumstances there is some choice available to us. Even in extreme cases, we can choose our response to the situation. Frankl (1986), who was interned in a Nazi concentration camp, points out that even in a concentration camp, no one has power over our beliefs, our attitudes and our values. Most of us are not faced with such extreme conditions, although some project leaders and managers in low- and middle-income countries work in very repressive contexts where their jobs and occasionally their lives may be at stake. We must refrain from judging those who choose to conform so that their own safety – physical, psychological or material – is maintained. If we have a family to feed and realise that there may not be other alternatives open to us, we may choose to remain employed in an oppressive work situation. If we do so with the idea that this is a choice we are making, we remain empowered. If we perceive ourselves as having no choice at all and having to stay in a work environment, as if this were a prison sentence, we will be dis-empowered. Psychologists have described a condition which they have named "learned helplessness" where people do not make any link between their own behaviour, attitudes, beliefs and actions and what happens to them.

Activity 5.7

Thinking about your project, is there evidence of learned helplessness? Do people generally feel dis-empowered?

Reframing: a powerful method for empowerment

I have mentioned earlier the importance of looking at situations from different perspectives. We can change a context by naming it different-ently. This method of reframing is a very powerful way of re-connecting with our own personal power and it enables us to be responsible. We can perceive a situation from many angles and from very different perspectives. We can choose to see an issue as a problem. To most of us a problem conjures up negative notions. However, we can decide to see the same issue as a challenge, which to many of us is more energising. But, better still, we can see this same thing as an opportunity to do something different and an opportunity to improve which moves us forward and is empowering.

Jonathan is the project leader in this refugee camp. The situation is desperate as these are refugees from a war zone who cannot go back home, at least not for a very long time. The project provides very basic health services. There is a multitude of problems. At first, Jonathan was very depressed. He is also angry and frustrated and he knows that many of the problems which are being encountered cannot possibly be resolved by the small projects operating in the camp. He even thought of abandoning the work and going home. But Jonathan has decided to stay; he discovered that he needed some challenges in his life and this is certainly a challenge. This reframing of the situation made Jonathan feel a little bit less helpless. It was energising to think that he was faced with the biggest challenge he had met so far in his life. Discussing this point with a colleague, he became aware of the opportunities he had. This transformation of an impossible problem into an opportunity has made Jonathan very enthusiastic about being here. He feels a surge of energy for his work and he is actively thinking out new strategies to adopt. He is discovering his own potential and also how creative he is. He is aware that this reframing would help his colleagues and the refugees. He is holding "workshops" with everyone who wishes to be involved in the camp to find out what opportunities they have, to find out what it is that people in the camp can do independently of outside organisations and agencies. This reframing has made the camp truly empowered.

Activity 5.8

Think of a problem you encounter. Reframe the same issue as a challenge. What opportunities does this issue present for you?

Writers on management (Pedler M. and Boydell T. 1985) point out that in any circumstance there are at least four choices: to change the situation if one has the power to do so, to change oneself and how one is reacting to the situation, to stay in the situation, accept it and deal with it as best we can, or to depart or withdraw from the situation. What this does for us is to make us realise that choice is involved. It is the perception of choice which causes people to remain empowered. Historically, many great leaders have shown us how this is the case. In recent years, people like Nelson Mandela have provided living examples. When he was in solitary confinement in Robben Island, he created choices for himself. For example, he chose to keep himself in very good physical condition by running on the spot in a very small enclosed area. Even when we are exposed to the worst abuse and people are attempting to humiliate us, we can choose to keep our own dignity and sense of self-respect. No-one can take this away from us.

When we come to believe that we are completely at the mercy of circumstances or of people, we have a sense of being controlled and we make ourselves powerless. By changing our belief and seeing our situation as one where we are not totally controlled and as one in which we have choices, we find that we can respond in several ways. The opposite of "learned helplessness" is to be empowered. We are empowered when we assume that we can exert choice and we can take decisions. Therefore, to ensure that we find out what choices we have is crucial to our work as project leaders. The more choice we believe we have, the more power we actually have.

Activity 5.9

Think about your own private life and list the constraints which you experience. Then list all the choices which you have in spite of the constraints you face.
Next, do the same exercise for your work situation. First of all, make a list of the constraints you face and then the choices you have in the midst of these constraints – and see how creative you can be about the choices open to you.

The above is a useful exercise to carry out any time we believe ourselves to be dis-empowered.

The dangers of passivity

When we feel helpless and powerless, we have a tendency to become passive and we fail to respond adequately to the situations we meet. There is an inclination to play a victim game, seeing ourselves as victimised and unable to help ourselves. This passivity arises from blaming what happens on an external cause or on our own inadequacies, from taking a fatalistic view or from believing that there is no hope at all in human beings. Sometimes, of course, people may display a mixture of the above. We learn to become helpless from having felt helpless in past situations. Passivity shows itself in by-standing as we take the passive role of lookers-on, i.e., we fail to act when we could do so. To redress this situation, we have to ensure that we take an active role and that we take part instead of being mere viewers.

How to deal with helplessness

There are different ways of dealing with helplessness. Sometimes we are able to influence the environment itself if we are in a position to change the possibility of the outcome in a situation. For example, in a case of conflict we can approach the situation by using a win-win rather than a win-lose perspective. What this means is that we do not set out to fight so that one side has to lose. We approach the situation in the same way as great negotiators do, by seeking to find out what is in it for the other. In this way, we discover the means by which the other person can be a winner as well as looking after ourselves so that we do not lose out. In so doing, we influence the outcome of the situation. Another means of dealing with helplessness is to become aware that it is not crucial for our survival to have the desired outcome; there are ways of surviving even if we do not get what we want.

Activity 5.10

Think of something which you would very much like to happen, e.g., passing an examination, getting a new post or a promotion etc. Consider the worst possible scenario in that situation, e.g., you fail your exam, you are not offered the job or the promotion. Then ask yourself the following questions:

– Can I survive if this worst possible scenario did come true?
– Is life bigger than my not achieving my desired outcome?
– What will I do if I do not get what I want?

Another method for curing helplessness is to face the inevitability of meeting some undesired and unavoidable events in life. We go back to the cyclical processes which we met earlier. In work and in life generally, we do meet things which we cannot possibly control and have to accept as being inevitable. Acceptance of what cannot be controlled is the wise thing to do.

Another way of dealing with powerlessness is to have positive expectations of what we want when the outcomes are actually realistic and within our grasp. This is another example of positive thinking. Many people hold a negative view of life. For example, when faced with an interview for a new job, they may keep saying to themselves that they are unlikely to be offered the post, that they are doomed to be treated unfairly and so on. If we approach a situation which is within our reach with a positive framework – believing that if it is the right thing for us we will actually be successful – we are much more likely to have a positive outcome. Of course, it does not mean that we will definitely obtain what we want, but the probability of this happening will be greatly increased.

Activity 5.11

Become aware of your thoughts. Notice the positive and the negative ones. Do not blame yourself when you have negative thoughts – simply observe what is happening and find ways of substituting these negative thoughts with positive ones.
Keep practising the above, and make it a regular habit to become aware of your thoughts.

Activity 5.12

Any time you would like to obtain a particular realistic outcome, do some affirmations on a regular basis and at the same time tell yourself that your survival does not depend on getting exactly what you would like.

In this last activity, note once again the existence of paradox. To increase the possibility of reaching an outcome, we have to wish for this outcome very much and at the same time let go of our desire.

Redressing the experience of helplessness leads in the long term to a greater sense of personal power and personal control. It also increases our feelings of self-esteem. We become more capable of dealing with uncertainty and complexity and are less likely to have bouts of utter helplessness.

About winners and losers

Winners are people who take responsibility for their lives and live in an authentic manner. They are genuine human beings who set out to achieve their potential and use the gifts that they have been given. They have many alternatives and know what to do if things do not work out the way they intended. Losers live their lives according to the prescriptions of others, they either do not achieve their stated purpose or if they achieve it, they are unhappy and uncomfortable with the outcomes. They are not authentic and are not true to themselves. They work and live according to what others have decided for them. They rely on one alternative, and have not worked out what to do if this is not successful. Their definition of success is a narrow one. For winners, success is not defined by others; to be successful means using one's talents and one's gifts for one's own personal development and for the benefit of society and the universe.

Peter is a senior manager. He has risen to this position through hard work. He has enjoyed some of it, but he generally feels very negative about his efforts. His aim in life seems to be that of pleasing authority figures. He decided that this was the way to climb the hierarchical ladders in the organisation for which he works. He has been promoted many times. After the initial pleasure from the promotion, he has always experienced dissatisfaction with his lot. He has dealt with this by working even harder and pleasing his managers in order to attain the next promotion. However, last year, a younger manager has been promoted to the post which Peter thought he would be given. He was totally unprepared for this and has been quite troubled since this happened. He blames his superiors for failing to notice how good a worker he is. He has no strategy to deal with "failures" and believes that he is a real failure in spite of the fact that he has attained a senior position. More importantly, Peter does not really know who he is. He changes his mind, he has different viewpoints according to whom he is trying to please. He is not even certain of what values and beliefs he holds. Peter is a loser.

Jessica is an authentic person who takes responsibility for her life. She did not benefit from all the educational opportunities which are available in the area where she lives as her parents were very poor and could not pay for the studies which she wanted to undertake. This did not deter Jessica. She started work in a job which she did not like at all. But instead of being unhappy, she decided that the job offered many opportunities for developing important skills. She studied at night school. This was an arduous and difficult time but Jessica did not complain, because she was so pleased to be able to undertake these studies. Since then, she has been able to move into a position which she very much likes. She continuously cultivates her talents. She is developing her potential, using her gifts and discovering new ones. She is known to be a genuine and honest person. Occasionally, her honesty has meant that she has been overlooked for promotion. Although Jessica was disappointed, she always had alternatives and has been able to pursue other avenues. She thinks of herself as highly successful – success in her eyes means developing and using her potential for herself and for the benefit of the wider society. Others do not think that she is successful as she has not been promoted to the level of other younger colleagues. Recently, she has surprised her colleagues by refusing a superior position. But to Jessica this was a wise decision, as she knows that the position offered is a mainly administrative one where she does not excel and this would take her away from her present field level position where she is fully able to use her aptitudes. Jessica is a winner.

Self-fulfilling prophecy

To follow on from the above discussion, we do know that the expectations we hold are very potent. To put it very simply, if we expect failure we tend to get failure, if we expect success, we get success. Therefore it is useful to make it a habit to anticipate success in everything we do – as long, of course, as we set ourselves realistic objectives. It also means that we have to re-define the inevitable "failures", as was discussed in a previous chapter, and reframe these as learning points. Self-fulfilling prophecies are very powerful and we need to become aware of how we personally create our own realities.

Pro-activity

In chaotic conditions, there are times when we cannot help but be re-active and we simply respond to circumstances. But as we are better prepared to deal with chaos and complexity, we become more pro-active. By developing the correct attitudes and enabling skills, we become enthused by uncertainty and complexity. We welcome the many opportunities given to us to develop our talents and to improve our creativity. We are prepared for what comes our way, we are ready for both good and bad times and we learn to discover the positive in the disasters, the trials and tribulations which we meet in our personal lives and in the workplace.

Authority

As managers, authority is a word which some of us dislike as it has come to depict abuse of power and misuse of the control which is given to us. Yet the word means to be the author of something. As project leaders, we need to rediscover the old meaning of this word and become the author, the creator and the initiator of our projects and of our lives. These are all energising concepts and we do need this energy, this force and this potency to be able to be effective and humane in our work. We also have to ask ourselves whether we allow others around us to be the "author" of their work, so that they can also be empowered.

The work instinct

Always you have been told that work is a curse and labour a mis-fortune.

But I say to you that when you work you fulfil a part of earth's
furthest dream, assigned to you when that dream was born,
And in keeping yourself with labour you are in truth loving life,
And to love life through labour is to be intimate with life's inmost
secret.

Kahlil Gibran (1992) *The Prophet*, Arkana Penguine Bookds,
London, pp. 35–36

If we have lost the work instinct, it is crucial for us to rediscover it
and its power. We need to distinguish between the "work ethic"
which sees work as duty and has done much harm to individuals and
the "work instinct" where work is a pleasure, a means of fulfilling
ourselves (Hillman J. in Moore T., 1990). When we are in touch
with the work instinct, we are truly in communion with our inner-
most self and also with the dreams of the universe. We re-discover
enthusiasm, excitement, exhilaration, ardour and eagerness. We re-
discover our own power, our own energy to contribute not only to
our development but to the development of others and to the development of the wider society.

On the importance of aspirations

And keep working. Exert yourself
toward the pull of God.
Laziness and disdain are not devotions.
Your efforts will bring a result.
You'll watch the wings of divine attraction
lift from the nest and come toward you!
As dawn lightens, blow out the candle.
Dawn is in your eyes now.

Rumi (1991) *One handed Basket Weaving. Poems of the Theme of
Work*, Versions by Coleman Barks, Maypop, Athens Georgia, p. 122

We also need to be aware of our dreams, our aspirations and our hopes and work towards them. When we yearn for something eagerly, we are much more likely to achieve it. What are our aspirations and our desires in our projects? To have those is very empowering. The wise project leader has dreams and aspirations and at the same time knows how to deal with the despair and the discouragement which appears when she is not able to attain her hopes and realise her desires. We meet paradox, i.e., the importance of really desiring something and the importance of having aspirations as well as the acceptance and the recognition that we may not be able to do/obtain what we so much desire. Part of achieving our dreams is to accept that in an imperfect world, we cannot be perfect. Seeking perfection is a recipe for failure: we are bound to fail. Discerning project leaders do their best, using their talents, developing their potential, living fully with all the energy and the enthusiasm which arise from the life force which is within all of us. They do not aim to be perfect but to be "good enough" leaders and managers.

Self- empowerment and being

We become self-empowered when we develop our "being" side, when we come to like ourselves unconditionally, just the way we are. When we are able to do so, we do not depend on external outcomes for our own self-esteem. We are able to withstand "failure", we are able to say "no" when this is the correct thing to do, even if this means that others may not like us for being assertive. As we discover the strengths of our inner self, we are much less at the mercy of outer goals and we are no longer at the mercy of others. The wise manager develops this inner self and discovers her strengths and resources. What happens at the same time is that through "being", our inner self becomes reflected around us in the "doing".

And, the more we are ourselves empowered, the more we are able to facilitate the development of others.

References and further reading

Clarkson P. (1992) *Introduction to Gestalt*, Sage, London.

Clarkson P. 1995, *Change in Organisations*, Whurr, London.

Frankl V. (1986) *The Doctor and the Soul*, Vintage Books, New York.

Gibran K. (1992) *The Prophet*, Penguin Books, London.

James M. and Jongeward D. (1971) *Born to Win*, Addison-Wesley, Wokingham.

Mulligan J. (ed.) (1988) *The Personal Management Handbook*, Sphere, London.

Moore T. (ed.) (1990) *The Essential James Hillman*, Routledge, London.

Megginson D. and Pedler M. (1992) *Self-development*, Mc Graw Hill, Maidenhead.

Pedler M. and Boydell T. (1985) *Managing yourself*, Fontana, London.

Rumi (1991) *One-handed Basket Weaving – Poems on the Theme of Work*. Versions by Coleman Barks, Maypop, Athens, Georgia.

Chapter 6   Facilitating the development of staff

The teacher who walks in the shadow of the temple, among his followers, gives not of his wisdom but rather of his faith and his lovingness.

If he is indeed wise he does not bid you enter the house of his wisdom, but rather leads you to the threshold of your own mind.

Kahlil Gibran (1992) *The Prophet*, Arkana Penguine Books, London, p. 74

The issue

We have seen the importance of continuous learning and constant change for projects. In the previous chapter, we have looked at the development of the manager which enables a situation of constant unlearning and learning. Here, we look at the manager's function in encouraging the development of workers. We consider the role of mentor and what this means for the management of individuals in the organisation.

Life positions

In our dealings with others, we can operate from four different life positions – see Table 6.1.

Table 6.1. Life positions (Ernst J. 1971)

I'm O.K. You're O.K.	I'm O.K. You're not O.K.
I'm not O.K. You're not O.K.	I'm not O.K. You're O.K.

These life positions refer to our fundamental beliefs about ourselves and people around us. We use them to support, rationalize and explain our decisions and our actions. The model is a complex one in that we may operate from different compartments in the core beliefs we hold, the behaviour we demonstrate to the world and the deep emotions which we feel. For example, someone whose behaviour is "I'm O.K. and You're not O.K." may in fact deep down believe that he is not O.K. The model, even when looked at superficially, as it is in this chapter, helps us understand our interactions with others. The healthy position is the "I'm O.K. – You're O.K." one, where we value ourselves and others. There is mutual respect for the dignity of human beings. Even when we disagree with the behaviour of someone else, we separate the person from the behaviour. From this position, there is a likelihood that we will be able to engage in a meaningful relationship with others. We are operating from a win/win view of the world, where there is no need to have a loser, and which leads to collaboration between people. In the "I'm O.K. – You're not O.K." mode, we see others as inadequate and as a result, we disparage them and engage in giving people put-downs; we are self-righteous, conceited, authoritarian and autocratic. In the "I'm not O.K. – You're O.K." position, we view ourselves as victims who are helpless in this world. We suffer from guilt and shame and become passive and submissive, unable to take care of ourselves, to venture into the unknown and to assume responsibility. The "I'm not O.K. – You're not O.K." stance is one of despair, of hopelessness where we are pessimistic, gloomy and cynical, seeing the worst in ourselves and in others. We view any action as futile when we are operating from this position.

Ideally, we need to operate from the "I'm O.K. – You're O.K." life position. Unfortunately, for us this is often not the case. We fluctuate and move from one life position to another – although individuals tend to have a dominant one. This model is useful in drawing our attention to the importance of functioning from the "I'm O.K. – You're O.K." position whenever possible, especially in our interactions with others in the workplace. It is not possible for us to operate from this ideal position all the time, because we are frail human beings for whom perfection is not possible. If we are tired, exhausted, stressed and experiencing low self-esteem or other life problems, there will be a tendency to revert to another life position. However, it is worthwhile to remind ourselves that whenever possible we should aim to be in an "I'm O.K. – You're O.K." position, especially when we are engaged in delicate interactions with members of staff, such as carrying out a staff appraisal.

Activity 6.1

At the end of each day, for a period of a week, keep a record of the life positions which you have used during the day.

– Review your record.
– Do you have a dominant life position?
– What can you do to ensure that you operate – at least for most of the time – from an "I'm O.K. – You're O.K." position?

Belief in the potential of workers

A starting point for managers and project leaders is to believe that workers are already, like them, quite competent people. They have acquired knowledge and many skills along the way. But in the same way that managers need to engage in a continuous learning process, they also would benefit from both personal and professional development. Work organisations gain from having valuable creative members. An important role is that of encouraging the development of workers. We start by holding the attitude that they are already quite adequate people. If we deem them to be deficient we would be operating from an "I'm O.K. – You're not O.K." mode in our dealings with them. To regard people as less able and inadequate inhibits learning by the learner. We learn best and improve our capacities much better when we already hold a very positive image of ourselves and see ourselves as undertaking a life-long learning process to develop our own potential as fully as possible. Similarly, it is vital that from the start we see our workers in the same light. If workers see themselves as deficient, the manager's function is to help them regain sufficient self-esteem so that they acquire the confidence to engage in unlearning and learning. Therefore the manager, as mentor, has faith in workers and provides them with love (agape) so that they can develop.

"Agape" – love in the workplace

We have seen in a previous chapter the importance of "agape" – altruistic love for others. With "agape", we may not like the other person at an emotional level and yet we have respect for her dignity and wish her well. It is what is meant when theologians talk of loving one's neighbour. Therefore, we may not feel affection for the other person but we desire and seek her well-being. The workplace is transformed when "agape" is present.

The essence of managing individuals effectively and humanely: unconditional love, empathy and authenticity

The essence of being able to manage people effectively and humanely involves the attitude and the belief system of the project leader. Rogers (1980) points out that in this "person to person" relationship, it is crucial to have unconditional love for the other person. This is the love of agape where we respect the dignity and the "being" of the other person regardless of what we feel towards this person emotionally and regardless of their "doing". In unconditional love, we care for the "being" of the other person. Having unconditional love for ourselves is an important starting point so that we are able to love others unconditionally, hence the importance of our own development and of our self-esteem as discussed in the previous chapter. Therefore, in spite of behaviour – the "doing" aspect – we perceive people as worthy of consideration and dignity – the "being" aspect. The aim is to differentiate between the "being" and the "doing" of others around us. The "being" needs our positive acceptance – we honour people's humanity unconditionally. The "doing" aspect includes the behaviour, the skills and the competencies, all of which can be improved.

Empathy for others is also important. This is an attempt to see the world from the perspective of the other. Of course, it is impossible for anyone to totally empathise with someone else – it is not possible for us to experience the world from someone else's viewpoint. However, we can do our utmost to do so, remembering that there are multi-perspectives and that the other's experience is valid even if we fail to understand that viewpoint.

In our dealings with others, it is important to be authentic and not engage in pretence. Our genuineness leads to sincere and unaffected relationship with others.

Activity 6.2

Reflect on your work organisation.

– **How are employees viewed and treated? Are there signs of respect for people as human beings?**
– **What can be done to ensure that people are treated in a humane and dignified manner?**

Recognition in the workplace

It appears that human beings crave attention and recognition. We prefer to be noticed, even in a negative manner, rather than not being acknowledged at all. In transactional analysis, the word ""stroke" is used to describe this phenomenon. This word has both positive and negative connotations; a stroke can be either a caress or a blow. The choice of this word with a double meaning brings to our attention the fact that people prefer to be recognised by others in a negative fashion rather than not be noticed at all. In work organisations, when workers do not get the attention they seek, they will behave badly so as to be acknowledged by their colleagues and their managers. Therefore, if we wish to encourage workers, a vital step is to give them sufficient attention. Giving feedback is, of course, a major and crucial form of strokes.

Activity 6.3

What sort of strokes are given to employees in your work organisation?

– **Do people receive mainly positive or negative ones?**
– **Is there any evidence of people seeking negative strokes because they are not receiving sufficient recognition?**

Conditional and unconditional strokes

We can give people different types of feedback: positive and negative ones. Strokes can be conditional – related to "doing" – and unconditional – referring to "being".

While we all need positive unconditional strokes, negative unconditional ones can be very damaging. Positive unconditional strokes affirm the whole person. We all require some positive unconditional strokes and it is important for us to have at least a few people who like and love us just the way we are. When we receive these affirmations, we experience warm feelings. Any time we value the whole person, or when we simply tell someone that we like him/her, we are giving positive unconditional strokes to that person.

Jenny is working for the first time in a primary health care project sponsored by the international NGO which employs her. She finds being so far away from home very difficult. She is also aware of learning on the job as she is meeting complex issues and situations for which she is unprepared. At times, she is very stressed and is unsure of herself and what she can contribute to the project. What keeps her enthusiasm is the way that she is appreciated by one of her colleagues and her project coordinator. They make it known that they like her as a person, although they are very aware of her lack of experience for the work which she is undertaking. Jenny realises that she has much to learn and welcomes the unconditional support which she receives. Although things are rather demanding and perplexing at times, Jenny remains confident that she will acquire the skills she needs for the assignment.

Negative unconditional strokes pass a verdict or a judgment about the whole person. To say "you are lazy, untrustworthy, etc." means that we are giving a label to someone else. We are failing to separate a behaviour, which we do not like, from the "being" of the other person. Unfortunately, in the long term, people tend to become the labels which have been given to them, as shown clearly by research work done by social scientists. This is an example of the power of the self-fulfilling prophecy. Negative unconditional strokes can seriously damage our self-esteem. Enabling managers refrain from giving negative unconditional strokes to people. However, we have all received these from other people. To maintain our self-esteem, it is crucial to refute them when they come our way so as not to assimilate the label. But we do have control on what we do to others. It is therefore important that managers ensure that they do not give negative unconditional strokes to others as we do not have the right to label negatively the "being" of another person. When we respect people, we ensure that we do not contribute to lowering their self-esteem and we apologise if we have inadvertently done so. Labels are rarely totally true. Even the so-called "lazy" worker works well at times when he is involved in and motivated by what he is doing. By labelling, we also adopt an "I'm O.K. – You're not O.K." stance as labels serve to distance ourselves from others. When we say to someone else "you are lazy", we imply that we are not lazy. In this way, we take on a superior attitude. Looking down on others as lesser beings who have these faults which we insinuate do not pertain to us.

Raj works as the medical assistant at the local government clinic. When he came to work there, he was full of enthusiasm. His manager is an authoritarian person who believes that things get done much better when he shouts. He is often abusive towards staff. Raj has been summoned to his office several times where the manager has accused him of being incompetent at his work. Raj is aware that there are many things about which he is unclear and he knows that he needs to learn to improve his technical abilities. However, he does not dare ask for advice – and sometimes he knows that he has made quite important mistakes because he was not sure what to do but did not want to ask. To him, asking for advice would confirm his manager's view that he is indeed incompetent. Raj is starting to have doubts about his suitability for the job. He no longer wants to come to work and has started to take time off sick any time he does not feel very well. This is a new pattern for him. He would like to change jobs, but there is not much work in the area and because of his family he believes that it would not be wise to move to another place at present. He is becoming very distressed as he knows that the quality of his work is not up to the standard that he himself would like. He is becoming uninterested and is starting to believe that he is indeed incompetent.

While negative unconditional strokes can be damaging for the person to whom they are directed, negative conditional strokes are very useful to us. When we want to change, to improve and ameliorate ourselves and our skills, the conditional feedback which we receive is very important. While unconditional strokes are concerned with the "being" of people, conditional strokes refer to "doing". Conditional negative strokes are vital to us so that we can develop. However, the manner in which they are given is also very important. To be constructive to the other, we have to be mindful of the way in which we give this type of feedback. When conditional negative strokes are given without "agape" love, the other person is likely to become defensive and will not hear what is being said. A few ground rules help in increasing the likelihood that the other person will hear our feedback. These are summarised in Table 6.2 below.

Table 6.2. Some guidelines for giving feedback

– Use the word "I", e.g., "I feel, I believe, I notice, I observe, etc."

– Do not pass judgment but describe the behaviour.

– Be as specific and as concrete as possible, e.g., say "I noticed that you were late for your clinic on two occasions last week and that patients were kept waiting – can we talk about that?"

– If possible, use a positive statement rather than a negative one, e.g., instead of saying "X and Y are missing in this report" say "you can improve this report by including X and Y."

To encourage workers to work well, a very powerful method is simply to give them plenty of positive conditional feedback. This tells people what they are doing well. When what we do well is acknowledged by others, we have a very strong tendency to repeat the behaviour. In addition, as mentioned earlier, giving unconditional positive feedback enhances the well-being of the other. This combination of conditional and unconditional positive feedback is a potent recipe for the development of people who work with us.

The timing of conditional feedback may influence the outcome. Positive conditional feedback is best given as soon as possible after the event. Then people are more likely to repeat the praised behaviour. Negative feedback is best given just before the person is about to repeat the behaviour which needs changing and, as stated earlier, this works better when done in a positive manner. Sports trainers use this method when they want to improve the skills of players. A football coach will say to players " I liked the way you did X and Y" as they are leaving the football pitch. They wait until a player is due to start a new training session and say "By the way, you can improve X by doing Z".

In work situations, the timing of feedback may be outside our control. What is entirely within our control is what feedback we give and how we give it to people around us.

As an aside, if we are not personally receiving sufficient positive feedback, the way to correct this is for us to be generous with giving positive feedback to others – we usually start receiving this ourselves; as the ancient saying affirms, what we give is what we receive.

We have all personally experienced the encouragement of receiving positive feedback and how this can re-kindle our enthusiasm when this has been waning. So, if we want to facilitate the development of workers, giving feedback is a valuable means of doing so.

Activity 6.4

– **What type of strokes do you personally receive?**
– **How do you deal with the unwanted negative unconditional ones?**
– **Are you able to refute them or do you come to believe the labels which people ascribe to you?**

- **How can you take care of yourself when you receive these?**
- **Do you receive sufficient positive unconditional and both negative and positive conditional strokes?**
- **What can you do if you do not receive enough of these?**
- **Are there people whom you could ask directly to give you more of these useful strokes?**
- **Think about all the positive strokes you could be giving to others around you.**
- **How good are you at giving those to people?**
- **Make a list of people to whom you can give positive feedback in the week to come. Start today and review your list at the end of the week.**

Self-fulfilling prophecies revisited

We saw earlier the power of self-fulfilling prophecies. Moreover, we have seen how labelling negatively can have formidable long-term outcomes. In the same way, positive labels are very powerful. The lesson for managers is that if we anticipate success, we obtain success. We have to reward the positive and recognize it, both formally and informally. If we pay attention to negatives, people will seek strokes through negative behaviour. Therefore it is crucial for us, whenever this is possible, to ignore the negative. Many people find it difficult to do so and are surprised that those around us keep seeking attention through negative patterns.

Change through modelling

The most effective way of encouraging others to learn is to be an excellent role model to them. We can only lead through example. We cannot suggest that people should behave in certain ways and not do so ourselves. The importance of starting with oneself has already been mentioned. We need to note it again here, as it is one of the most important determinants of successful learning.

Healing the injury of previous learning

For many people, the experience of education has been a painful one. Too often, the conventional educational system has thwarted the natural curiosity which we all had as children, because the young child is always eager to learn. Rigid rules, stern and austere teaching, emphasis on rote learning and on logical thinking have also inhibited the innate creativity which we see in very young children as yet untouched by the formal system. As managers, we have to remember that many workers have been damaged by previous learning and by a shaming culture. Our role is to revitalise their enthusiasm for learning and help them re-discover their creativity. The good news for managers as educators is that any positive educational experience in the present to some extent helps in healing past educational trauma.

On being a mentor

There are teachers who nurture us but stifle our independence, our initiatives and our autonomy. They turn out to be very caring but they have a propensity to make things easy for us, to protect us from difficulties and stop us from meeting our own adversities, our own hurdles and our own tribulations. Other teachers are real mentors. They also care for us and guide us. However, unlike the first type, they allow us to discover our own path. They allow us to make mistakes because it is through making our own mistakes that we learn best. They intervene only if there is a danger either to ourselves or to others by our actions and non-actions. They are real guides to us on our journey through life. The manager who wants to facilitate learning, needs to be the mentor who allows others to find their own paths and that includes learning from mistakes. People learn more from doing things wrong. This is how we build up our self-confidence. Confidence accrues when we find ways of getting up again after falling down, when we discover how to correct the errors. The mentor's role is to permit these situations to happen, to support peo-

ple while they are experiencing difficulties and to reveal to employees the attractions and the advantages of continuous learning.

The mentor has a valuable guiding role, but she does not strive to
have people leaning constantly on her in a dependency position.
Instead she inspires and encourages others to move towards autonomy,
rediscovering their own strengths and abilities so that they can guide
themselves through the chaos of life and work.

The outcome of learning: celebration of differences

As we have just seen, we need managers to be real mentors who
allow people to make their own journey. An important aspect of this
is not to expect others to believe exactly what we believe, to have
the same ideas, thoughts and values as ourselves. Effective mentors
allow others to be different, if that is what they choose to be. These
are the teachers whom workers require in an organisation. They
need managers to be genuine mentors who do not use educational
strategies as a means of indoctrination.

Too often, when managers take their role as educators seriously, they
attempt to coerce workers to see the world from their own perspectives. From this viewpoint, the successful outcome of the educational
process consists of everyone sharing the same values, beliefs and opinions. This is not education but indoctrination. Besides, as we have seen
in earlier chapters, this is not conducive to thriving in a chaotic world.
For work organisations to be effective, we have to value and celebrate
differences.

To be authentic mentors to others, as managers we need to be aware
of the propensity of human beings to simply comply. In an experi-
mental research series done by psychologists, they showed how "normal" human beings had no qualms about obeying orders (Milgram, S.
1974). In a disguised experiment, people were urged by the researcher
to administer electric shocks to others posing as subjects. The great
majority of people – very ordinary, educated and "normal" – simply
obeyed and when asked to do so by an authority figure, increased the
dose of electric shock regardless of the pain of "victims". Very few
chose to abandon taking part in the experiments. It seems that human

beings comply very readily with someone who is seen as a higher authority. In the workplace, we have to be conscious of this inclination of people to blindly obey and submit to those who rule and command. Workers generally do their utmost to please managers and others in authority. By so doing, they may not be serving the best interests of themselves, of the project or of the organisation. As we shall go on to see in the following chapter, successful work organisations in the face of chaos celebrate differences and encourage conflict, because they know that conflict and differences are potentially very creative.

Leadership styles

Different leadership styles are available when dealing with people: managers can move along a continuum from a hierarchical style through a cooperative one to an autonomous style at the end of the continuum (Heron, J. 1990). In the hierarchical mode, the leader takes decisions and directs people. Here, power is exercised **over** people. There are many times when this style is the appropriate one to use in managing a project. In the context of helping the development of others, this style is useful with people who have been so damaged by past educational experience that they cannot manage without an overt leader. At times, the distress of a group is so profound that we have to take on the hierarchical model – with the group as dependent on us. If we choose this style, it is crucial that we become conscious of what we are doing so that we do not encourage dependency which would indubitably not lead to empowerment in the long term. In the early days of working with a group which is in the dependency mode, it may be wiser to take on the hierarchical style to make the group feel safe enough. However, to stay in that style would not be appropriate for the long-term development of the group members. In the cooperative mode, authority is shared between the leader and others. Here, power is exercised <u>with</u> others. In work organisations, there are many opportunities for this style of leadership. Especially when decisions involve others, it is important to use this style of leadership where solutions to issues are found in conjunction with those affected.

The autonomous mode is the one where others are so empowered that they do not need us. Here, authority has been delegated to people who take their own decisions. Those with whom we work have power and, as leader, we support and respect the exercise of power by them.

This delegation of power should not be done in a manipulative, suffocating and patronising manner. It involves generating the circumstances where people can exert their autonomy to satisfy their own needs of independence and to fulfil the requirements of the task at hand.

As mentors, we hope that our workers will be autonomous beings. If they maintain too much dependence, we may need to challenge them. Not to do so will help neither these people nor the work organisation.

All three leadership styles have their place when we manage other people. We need to be aware of the style we are currently using by asking ourselves whether this style is appropriate to the situation.

Activity 6.5

Assess your leadership styles.

– Which ones do you use and when?
– Are the styles appropriate to the people and the context in which you are operating?
– Check out with other people whether the styles you use are suitable or not.

The servant leader

This terminology of servant leader was coined by a successful manager, Robert Greenleaf (1977), to point out that leaders in organisations are there to serve others. This paradox of being both leader and servant at the same time, demonstrates the need for leaders to be there to attend and assist people and facilitate their efforts in work organisations. To be able to do so, we require humility about our roles; we need to listen carefully to those who work with us and be attentive to their needs and their development.

The ethics of influencing others: indoctrination or education?

In social life, we cannot not influence others. Whether we intend to or not, our actions or non-actions invariably have some effect on those around us. We are all interconnected. How we use this influence raises ethical issues. We can choose to educate in the wider sense of the word, where the other is left free to take or leave what we have to say, the emphasis being on the autonomy of the learner. In manipulation, we intentionally use our influential power to coerce directly or indirectly someone else for our benefit and not that of the other. Manipulation is easy to use in the workplace, especially where employers are only concerned with productivity and their aim is how to make the most from employees without any regard for them as people. This can happen in a very subtle manner, under a cover of caring for others. It is important to face the ethical issues raised when we possess the skills necessary to encourage others to change. Are we seeing to the person with due respect for human dignity when we are also at the same time wanting to improve productivity? An important difference between manipulation/indoctrination and real education is that in the former we are not at all pleased when learners do not follow our ways and do not adhere to our perspectives. This is not so in real education; there, what we are looking for is someone who thinks critically. In true education, the outcome may be that learners reject everything which we have to say and we accept their right to do so. There is an important power differential between managers and employees. It is crucial that managers do not abuse the power they have over others.

The meaning of support

Support is an important aspect of encouraging others in their own learning and development. However, what we mean by this word is rarely made explicit. There is no doubt that human beings thrive in a supportive rather than a punitive environment. The support of managers is very important to workers. They feel valued as people and know that they can get the help they require. Support is therefore about caring and about nurturing. But this is not sufficient and people need other things. They require adequate information to be able to do their job well. This does not mean that all information has to be transmitted to staff. Too much information can be problematic and no one wants to receive irrelevant material. But appropriate and pertinent information needs to be communicated to staff.

To be able to fully develop and explore their potential, as discussed above, people have to be encouraged to confidently undertake their own "odyssey". They can only do so in the workplace if they are given sufficient opportunities for experience. Delegating the right job to the right person is a skillful activity. To allow people to thrive, we have to provide experiences which will stretch their abilities, which will help in developing new skills but which are not beyond their capabilities, otherwise they will be discouraged.

But there is also another important element to support and this is challenging support. To be able to develop and to grow, we have to be challenged. Positive confrontation and challenge can be very energising and help us re-connect with our creativity and our life-force.

The best way of motivating people is through this paradoxical type of support which is at the same time accepting, nurturing, caring and also confronting and challenging.

Activity 6.6

– **Is there sufficient caring and nurturing as well as challenging support in your work organisation?**
– **Do people receive the right amount and the appropriate information?**
– **What can be done to improve support and the dissemination of information in your workplace?**
– **What action can you personally undertake? How and when will you implement this action?**

Dealing with anxiety in the workplace

As we have seen previously, living and working in a complex and uncertain world leads us to feel anxious. We need to be aware of the anxiety – both explicit and unspoken – in work organisations and have sufficient safety for people to be able to function at the edge of chaos. Acknowledgement of our fears and anxiety is an important starting point. As leaders, we have to find out how to provide sufficient security for workers, because, paradoxically, we need enough safety to be able to take risks.

Clarifying the nature of the working alliance

When we work, we have a contract with our employers. The nature of this contract needs to be clear. All work organisations have many rules about issues, although these may not be made explicit to people. These need to be made clear. They also have to be flexible and change according to circumstances. It is crucial that we state what these are. People have to know what is totally unacceptable, what is negotiable and what is entirely within their discretion and authority.

Activity 6.7

Think about a specific post in your organisation.
Work out what is:

(1) unchangeable and unacceptable
(2) negotiable
(3) entirely within this person's discretion and authority

Elements which damage staff development

People are damaged in the workplace when they are exposed to blame, sarcasm, shame and humiliations. They also become incapacitated when they are expected to perform unrealistically. When a work organisation has utopian aims or expects employees to deliver the impossible, they will become alienated.

Much harm is done when there are poor relationships in a work setting, when there are personal attacks on people, when there is unpleasant interpersonal conflict with people getting hurt, where there is violence in the way in which people are treated and where there is no respect for the humanity of others. It is also difficult for people to sustain themselves in settings where they are not included and feel isolated. In this type of situation, people do not feel safe and are unable to give the best of themselves. Their energy is invested in protecting themselves from the harm which is being done to them.

Mary is a social worker who has been asked to join a team of doctors and nurses working in a community project. The existing staff did not want a social worker in their team; this has been imposed by the Regional Medical Officer. Mary used to work with supportive colleagues in an atmosphere of mutual respect and trust where the emphasis was on cooperation between people.

She is totally bewildered by the behaviour of her new colleagues. Staff meetings are the sites for personal attacks, blame and ridicule, with colleagues engaging in putting down others any time there is an opportunity to do so. The project leader has totally unrealistic expectations about what she can achieve. No one really understands her work and she feels isolated and is starting to distance herself from her colleagues in an attempt to protect herself. Mary used to be a very creative person who worked well and was esteemed by both colleagues and clients. She is keen that her clients should not suffer and does what she can to ensure that she does a good job, in spite of the difficulties which she now faces. But her health is suffering very badly. She is often weepy and feels continuously drained and exhausted. She is thinking of finding a new post elsewhere.

Supporting groups in the workplace

The extensive literature on group dynamics draws our attention to the fact that dealing with individuals is not the same as dealing with groups. Groups have their own patterns and their own identities. The work group is very influential in what gets done and what does not get done. Moreover, generally people wish to belong to the social setting. The social needs of people are very important in the workplace. Issues of inclusion/exclusion, control and affection are played and re-played throughout the existence of the group. Some individuals have difficulties with getting themselves included and at the same time, the group may actively exclude people, especially those who do not conform to the dominant group norms. Groups expect conformity and deviants have a difficult and painful time. These deviants may be the most creative people in the organisation, as we know that by nature, very creative people tend to be non-conformists. As managers, we may have to facilitate the inclusion of people.

Influencing others and exerting control over others is another vital issue in groups. Sometimes control is exerted by very few people while others remain passive and become by-standers. For the effective functioning of a group, we need to see that all members, at some time, have an opportunity to exercise some influence on what goes on, otherwise we may lose out on potentially very useful contributions.

Affection between people is another concern in the life of a group. Time spent during official work hours on social activities is time well spent, as long as this is well balanced with time devoted to carrying out the task in hand.

Groups which are functioning well continuously recycle dealing with the issues of inclusion/exclusion, power/influence and affection, taking greater risks each time and revealing more about themselves. In this way, high trust levels can develop between people. Non-effective groups have ceased recycling these issues and have become static. People feel dissatisfied and unhappy and may terminate their active participation in the group. If team work is important for the organisation, the manager has to intervene to re-stimulate interest and enthusiasm in the group.

Another important function for project leaders is that of managing the boundaries between the social and task aspects of the group. If an organisation is too task-focused, there is not sufficient bonding between people and we find groups and not teams. If the organisation is too people focused, we may find very happy people, getting on well together, enjoying each other's company but with the task being neglected. Managing groups involves ensuring that both the social and the technical parts of the system receive sufficient time, attention and energy.

Activity 6.8

Reflect on your working group.

- **Are they recycling the inclusion/exclusion, power/influence and affection sequence?**
- **How much time, effort and energy is spent on the technical aspect of the work organisation, how much is spent on the social aspect?**
- **Do you think that you have the correct balance between the two? If not, what can you do to redress the balance?**

Unconscious processes in the group

The work of Bion at the Tavistock Institute in London (1961) draws our attention to common unconscious processes which sometimes facilitate but often may hinder the work of a group. These are the strategies of fight/flight, pairing and dependency.

These can be linked to very deep and primal fears.

In fight/flight, group members are involved either in fighting each other or the leader or in flight – either physically or psychologically. In the latter example, they may be physically present but mentally absent from the work organisation. Pairing refers to energy being focused between two people – who might engage in high levels of communicating/acting while the rest of the group looks on. In dependency, the group behaves as if they were children and crave for dependency, usually on the leader. In all three, energy is spent on the strategies with much less or very little effort being put into carrying out the task. These tactics when used negatively, stop people from being fully developed adults acting on the basis of personal responsibility, choice and autonomy, which constitute the core of being self-empowered.

Activity 6.9

Is there any evidence of the fight/flight, pairing and/or dependency phenomena in your work organisation?

- **Do these strategies facilitate or hinder the work?**
- **If these exist in the organisation, what is causing the underlying anxiety?**
- **What can you do to relieve this anxiety and create a climate where people feel empowered?**

Valuing people

The main intervention in developing people in the work place is to value them. This shows that we respect their humanity and we are operating within the empowering transaction of the "I'm O.K. – You're O.K." framework. Valuing people says to them that we believe that they are worthy of deference. In this way they maintain sufficient self-esteem and confidence and are better able to flourish and become more creative.

On the importance of our own attitude

To enable others to empower themselves means, in effect, that interventions are quite minimal (we shall look at this issue in greater detail in a later chapter on being a change agent). The main change is not at the level of action, but concerns a change in attitude: attitude towards others and having a positive frame of mind. We meet another example of reframing. It is the difference between people who delight in the fact that thorns bear roses, rather than those who lament that roses have thorns. It is very much about how we choose to look at our settings and how we choose to view people.

The empowerment myth

Professionals often talk of empowering others. We cannot cause someone else to be empowered through an intervention. Individuals and groups have to choose to empower themselves. When the power relationship is a very unequal one, the only way for subordinate groups to gain more power is for them to seize it. History shows that those in power do not give it away – it has to be taken. We take power in a context of inequality by taking part – by refusing the passive role of the bystander. Therefore, we have to encourage our employees to become involved, to take part in the processes and the conversations of the organisation. We cannot insist that they do so but we can help them along the path. When they stop being mere by-standers, they discover their own power and are able to act responsibly. Our role therefore is one of providing the correct environment where it is easier for others to empower themselves.

The aim for managers is to make people around them aware of the importance of continuous learning and unlearning. Part of this process is to encourage people to discover and get in touch with their own personal power. This is mainly achieved through the manager herself being a good role model. In the previous chapter, we have discussed how crucial it is to start with one's own development. The best way to manage is to lead by example. Through modelling, many around us start to internalise useful means and skills for dealing with the uncertain and chaotic world in which we work. Another crucial role for the manager as mentor is that of providing an environment conducive to development where people are nurtured, where anxiety is dealt with, where there are good relationships between people and where clear and open communication takes place.

We need an environment which is safe enough for people to participate fully, where they are praised not only for what they do well but also for taking risks and for not being afraid of making mistakes. We have to provide a setting where employees engage in creative conflict and disagreement while respecting each other as human beings. Therefore what happens in the organisation is crucial to whether or not our best resources, people, have opportunities to develop their potential and capacities. We therefore have to ask whether the organisation fosters or hinders empowerment. The next chapter looks at the organisation, its culture and what is required to support learning and unlearning in the face of complexity and uncertainty.

References and further reading

Bion W.R. (1961) *Experience in Groups and other Papers*, Tavistock, London.

Clarkson P. (1994) *The Achilles Syndrome*, Element Books, Shaftesbury, Dorset.

Ernst Jr. F.H. (1971) The OK Corral: The Grid for 'get-on-with'. *Transactional Analysis Journal* 1 (4): 33–42.

Gibran Kahlil (1992) *The Prophet*, Penguin Books, London.

Greenleaf R.K. (1977) *Servant Leadership*, Paulist Press, New York.

Heron J. (1990) *The Facilitators' Handbook*, Kogan Page, London.

Milgram S. (1974) *Obedience to Authority*, Harper and Row, New York.

Rogers C.R. (1980) *A Way of Being*, Houghton Mifflin, Boston.

Chapter 7   The unlearning and learning organisation

The issue

To have successful projects we need not only managers and workers who are constantly learning but also an organisation which facilitates this. We can look at organisations as if they have their own identity. The study of organisational behaviour shows clearly that work organisations have their own cultures and modes of behaving. This is not so extraordinary as organisations are simply large groups. In the same way as we can observe patterns of "being" and "doing" among a small group of people interacting together which is separate and different from the individuals who make up that group, we also have ways of "being" and "doing" in organisations. We need to remember what has been said in an early chapter that organisations are about interactions and the relationships we have with people and it is in this interacting that we construct the organisation.

This chapter will focus on the work organisation and explore the components of an organisation engaged continuously in unlearning and learning.

The importance of culture

The culture of an organisation refers to the underlying assumptions, the values, the beliefs the attitudes which profoundly affect and permeate everything the organisation undertakes. In work organisations, culture is rarely made explicit but has pivotal influence. We recognise the culture by observing what goes on in the organisation; for example, the style of the offices, the type of clothes people wear, the way they spend their time, the pace of work, what is talked about and what is not said, etc., reveal the culture. The components of culture are therefore often tacitly understood and taken for granted.

A significant feature of culture is that it is a dynamic process; culture is not static, it is forever changing. We are affected by culture and in the same time we change and mould the culture. Therefore, paradoxically the culture of an organisation exists outside us and at the same time we create it. Therefore there is an interrelationship between the culture and us as individuals, with people re-shaping and re-formulating the culture. Organisational culture gives us patterns of shared meanings. These shared meanings and assumptions generate cohesion which is a useful thing in that it binds people together. The strongest element in integrating an organisation and in fostering the union of people who work there is the organisational culture. However, there is another side to this phenomenon. Culture leads to integration, to cohesion and to stability and it is also one of the most important obstacles to change. This impediment to progressive change is often hidden from us as we take the culture of our organisation for granted and we rarely query its usefulness to us.

This international NGO was started in the 1960s with the aim of providing emergency relief to countries of the South. It has traditionally recruited young people seeking adventure but with much dedication and enthusiasm for the work they undertake. It has a high media profile which helps in recruiting new people. The picture which it presents to the outside world accurately reflects the internal culture. It shows itself as an organisation which does not fear to go to difficult, complex and sometimes dangerous situations. The public image is one where workers are devoted to the disadvantaged, being themselves slightly outside the wider society, adventurous spirits with much courage and a sense of heroism. When people come to work for the organisation, they find what they are seeking: adventure, excitement, a spirit of camaraderie and a sense of being different from the "boring" people who make up the majority of the society in which they live. But on the ground they also discover that they are only human beings. Like the rest of us, they experience fear in difficult circumstances. They become distressed by the work they undertake. They feel unprepared for the level of despair they meet in their work. They are very highly stressed but cannot admit it as this would be seen as a sign of weakness by the organisation. At the level of the organisation, managers deny that workers are stressed when the subject is brought up by the few people who dare say that which remains unspoken by all the others. These few people feel very frustrated and are thinking of leaving the organisation.

Majeed works for a government department, part of the Ministry of Health. He has just returned from a course abroad, full of enthusiasm and with many new creative ideas for the projects which he coordinates. The offices of the Ministry where he is based reflect the underlying culture. Everything in every room is simply utilitarian. There is nothing attractive about the place, which is badly kept. In each office, one can see stacks of papers piled high. It seems that one way of showing one's status is to have as many of these heaps of paper as is possible. In public, everyone looks very busy, rushing around in the corridor, although in private it seems that many people are wasting precious time. When one enters an office unexpectedly, the occupant is often busy on a long personal conversation on the telephone. There are endless meetings. Days are full of meetings and committees to attend. There is evidence of activity and busy-ness but not much to show in terms of outcome.

Majeed has brought up the issue of change in staff meetings. He has met with much resistance. Finally, his manager has agreed that he should start a new working party with the idea of having several committees to look at the issues which he wants the organisation to address.

Activity 7.1

If a total stranger arrived in your work organisation, what would they notice as striking?
Ask a friend to visit you at your workplace, and find out what they see to be noticeable and surprising. Make sure you get their first impressions as these are often very revealing.
List the characteristics of your work setting.

- **What is disclosed by the physical layout, by what people wear, by what they do?**
- **What are the taboos, what are the secrets in your work organisation?**
- **What are the implications of the culture for individuals and for the performance of the task?**

Power, culture and organisations

In most work organisations, there is substantial inequality of power between individuals. Power in itself is neither good nor bad; it is the way that power is exercised which is important. For example, we need hierarchies but the way that these function may be problematic if those who are higher up in the hierarchy manipulate and are unjust and unfair to those lower down.

Power inequalities interrelate with the culture of an organisation. Everyone, to some extent, creates and re-creates culture but those who have the most power have more opportunities to determine for others what will be considered important or not. They are also able to impose their own beliefs, assumptions and values on others, who of course do not have to accept these passively and can (and do) resist.

Therefore, those who have the most power in an organisation – and managers have more power than ordinary employees – are able to draw the lines around the boundaries, about what is possible, what is inadmissible and what is unchangeable.

The amount of power we have or do not have determines the roles we can or cannot play. The culture of an organisation can be used to create and sustain unequal power relationships and therefore culture can be used as a strong means of controlling people.

This primary health-care project was started by a small group of devout Christians. The project is still managed by these founders who maintain a strong control over all aspects of the project. People who come to work for the project are expected to have a religious idea of service and to be totally committed to the project. Prayer is an important means of creating cohesion in the project. Some employees complain about the conditions of work and are inevitably told that they are not good Christians because good ones have a strong dedication to service and are on this earth to serve the poor and not to care for themselves.

Pat has recently taken up work as a secretary in this well-known international NGO. She used to work for the private sector but now that her children are grown up, she finds that she does not need the salary she earned. She would like to do her part for the disadvantaged in this world.

Therefore, she took up this new post although the salary is much lower. She is an enthusiastic woman who has developed many interests outside work and sees these activities as very important. She also believes that it is crucial for her to have some quiet, reflective time. She is very much enjoying work at the NGO. However, she is having difficulties with the hours of work. Pat believes in leaving the office on time but everyone else works very long hours. When she did leave on time people remarked on it. Meetings, which she is expected to attend, are held outside official working time. As a newcomer, Pat does not quite know what to do. She believes that she has to be careful about what she says. She has even started to feel slightly guilty whenever she leaves the office on time as her colleagues are inevitably still very busy in the office. Although Pat likes being here, she is already thinking that she might have to give up this job and go and work once again for the private sector.

Culture, power and change

If we want to profoundly alter an organisation, we need to change its culture. Of course this is the most resistant to change – it is what gives the organisation its unique flavour and identity. But we can change culture. As we said earlier, although we are strongly affected by the culture of an organisation, we can also take an active part in re-creating the culture. What change we can effectuate depends on our position in the organisation and in the following chapters we shall focus on the topic of change. What we need to note here is that anyone, whatever his or her position, can engage in some sort of change. We can realize the change which is within our power and within our control. For example, by just working differently, we are at some level affecting the system. I am not suggesting that one person can change a large system. However, one person doing things differently will have some effect, at least on a small part of the organisation. We do not know in advance what ripple effect this small change may have on the wider system. We need to guard against being a bystander if we do not like the culture of our work organisation. Complexity theory shows us that we cannot not take part, that every part is interrelated, and that although we cannot con-

trol the future, we can influence it. We are co-creators of that future;
hence the question becomes "what am I personally doing to change
that which I do not like?" Blaming others is not helpful.

Managers as culture workers

As the culture of an organisation or a project is so crucial to what
gets done and what does not, managers have a role in creating and
sustaining a culture which facilitates rather than hinders effective
work and satisfactory personal relationships. For example, many
work organisations are driven by a shame culture where the name of
the game is that of shaming and trying not to be shamed in return.
Shame cultures are very detrimental to growth, development, learning and creativity.

Managers can have an influence in changing destructive cultures.
They can choose to be culture workers in their organisation, taking
note of the culture of the organisation, considering the implications of
that culture and facilitating any change which they have power to
undertake. Later on, in this book, we look closely at the change
process and what it means to be a change agent. Here, we concentrate
on looking at the characteristics of an organisational culture which
supports unlearning and learning.

The organisation at the edge of chaos

Effective organisations, as we saw in the beginning of this book,
avoid operating at the two extremes of the continuum, i.e., ossification and disintegration. They embrace the position at the edge of
chaos as much as possible. Here, we consider a few characteristics
of organisations which are at the chaotic edge.

A tension between stability and instability
As we have seen before, in the chaotic edge we meet paradox and
opposites are present at the same time. Organisations which perform

well in conditions of uncertainty and complexity have a healthy tension between stability and instability, between order and disorder. There is much order and stability in the day-to-day running of the organisation. For example, there are good systems to deal with the routine of administration. There are clear rules and procedures about the predictable and the habitual. People in the organisation have good methods for dealing with anything which is both relatively simple and certain.

At the same time, there is instability and disorder. There is much discussion in corridors, in kitchens and in the coffee area. Staff are encouraged to spend time in these places. At staff meetings, people are very challenging of authority and of what goes on in the organisation. There are dreams and ideas about what people want to achieve and where the project aims to go, but no rigid plans and procedures. Strategy is allowed to emerge and people in the organisation work with that which emerges rather than with what they had decided should happen.

The basis for any future action is one which takes into consideration the aspirations of people and those of the wider organisation. But no one knows exactly what will happen in the future. This "let's see how it goes" style of working is found side-by-side with regular monitoring which takes place systematically on a very regular basis.

This international NGO has recently instituted a new project to help local workers move from a mainly institution-based service for the disabled to one which is more community-based. It has now been operating for about 6 months and the project is funded for 5 years. People in the NGO have implemented some useful systems. There is much administrative work involved with communications across communities, different organisations in-country as well as internationally. A good and effective information system has been installed to help. An administrator with much experience of office systems coordinates the work; he has instituted clear procedures for some of the administrative work as well as organising plans for budgeting and for financial issues. The project leader has set up a method for systematic monitoring. The results of the monitoring activities are reported to all involved at regularly held formal meetings. The funders want to know exactly what will be the end results of the project. The project leader has given them some out-

comes, which he is fairly confident will be met. He has agreed with the funders that he will provide them with 6- monthly reports but he wants some of the important outcomes to be very flexible. He prepared a paper which he sent to the funding bodies. In this he showed how he would like this project to run. The aim is to avoid a top-down approach and he wants to consult with interested agencies, people and organisations. He sees his task as mainly that of facilitating a process rather than that of telling people what to do. In the early days of the project, staff did very little. For much of the time they sat around in the community attending the markets where the women are to be found and spending time talking to them. They are also often seen drinking the locally brewed beer in the village at the spots where the men meet. They attend most of the activities of local organisations concerned with the disabled. They have also organised many parties to which many of the people concerned have been invited. Visiting this project one can see the enthusiasm on people's faces, they are having fun but can produce the documents visitors request. Much of the process is systematically documented and reviewed. At the end of 6 months they are just starting to get a feel for what the project is all about. There are issues about training local people and about changing attitudes towards disability. Although professionals are enthusiastic about the idea of community-based rehabilitation, many mothers of disabled people have voiced serious reservations. They do not feel that the time they have will allow them to take on the extra care of their children which a community-based approach suggests. The major point, it seems, is how to make the care of disabled children the responsibility of a whole community and not to give an extra burden to the mothers of these children. Another important issue is to investigate what role disabled people can and will take. The project leader is confident that solutions will emerge. Meanwhile, he encourages people to meet casually and does not expect anyone to tell him exactly what their plans are.

In the effective organisation subversion is encouraged

An important characteristic of the organisation at the chaotic edge, not often seen in many work organisations in low- and middle-income countries, is that subversion is not only tolerated but actively encouraged. This demands managers who have enough self-esteem and who operate mostly from an "I'm O.K." position. If this were not so, managers would feel very threatened by subversive activities in their projects; hence another significance of personal development for the individual manager. Counter-cultures force us to see what is problematic in the dominant culture and thus assist learning and unlearning. We need this challenge to be able to confront our deeply held beliefs and ideas. I discussed earlier how culture helps in bringing about cohesion and in binding people together. This also means that a strong culture stops us from changing and prevents us from unlearning and learning. Culture is to a large extent hidden from us, as it is what we take for granted and we fail to question the basic assumptions which guide our way of viewing the world. Therefore, we do not see what needs to be changed, what may be inappropriate and what is no longer helpful to us. There is a tendency to keep the culture as it is. When we have sub-cultures which are different from the dominant one, we are able to see the realities of our own culture. Anthropologists have used this device to understand their own cultures and societies. It is by their looking at very different contexts that they can illuminate their own cultures and their own societies. The advent of more widespread travelling to foreign parts also has this effect. By visiting another land, not only do we discover the quaint ways of others but we also uncover what is strange about ourselves. Counter-cultures help us see what needs to change. They also help in disrupting the field, by causing enough instability for change to occur – a topic which we will discuss at greater length in another chapter when we look at the change process.

The creative conflict which is spurred by counter-cultures helps in the de-struction which is required before we can re-construct. Thus, subversion is useful in that it stimulates an organisation to un-learn in order to be able to move into a new learning phase.

Activity 7.2

– Are there counter-cultures in your workplace?
– How are these counter- cultures handled?
– Are they encouraged or are they subdued and suppressed?
– What can you learn from any existing counter-cultures?

Self-organising groups

As we have seen, an important element of complex systems is the way that agents spontaneously form self-organising groups. These form in an unplanned manner, unlike formal working groups and committees. Self-organising groups hold conversations, and new forms emerge in these interactions. Self-organisation can operate along fixed patterns or at the chaotic edge. When they occupy this transition phase between order and disorder, creative ideas materialise. The significant factor about these groups is that they are self-forming and self-organising. Therefore we cannot organise self-organising groups! In the same way we cannot predict whether this spontaneous self-organisation, which is happening all the time, will lead to creative emergence at the chaotic edge or will repeat fixed patterns.

   As managers, we cannot order people to be creative and innovative. This is not how creativity is generated. But we have a role in providing the environment where there is a greater likelihood that workers will be creative and will engage in continuous learning. One way of doing so is to encourage people meeting, interacting and holding conversations with each other in an informal and messy manner in our projects. It is through the interactions and the conversations which take place that strategies emerge. In some work organisations, the formal structure and its managers do their best to disband the formation of informal groups engaging in conversations and to thwart their activities. Many organisations in the private sector have known for a long time that real decisions and creative ideas are produced from these informal gatherings; hence, the meetings in the bar, on the golf course, etc. To stimulate these activities, we can facilitate and encourage informal meetings of people in and outside the premises of the organisation. Often people self-organise around an issue and when this issue has been resolved, the membership of the group breaks up. When another issue emerges, another self-organising group materialises. The manager's role is to facilitate the advent of these self-organising groups but she cannot and must not control its membership, what it chooses to do and what culture it wishes to adopt. It seems important to keep repeating that we do not organise the self- organisation of people. We need simply to recognise its importance and to take part in that activity and not dismiss this as not-work.

However, managers can encourage the existence of creativity groups to enhance people's skills in decision-making, to facilitate their functioning in groups and to generate ideas. In many organisations, these learning groups have been found to be very useful. For example, in multi-sectorial work, people from various sectors can be invited to join creativity groups where people engage in creative decision-making and problem-solving through meaningful conversations and dialogue. The manager sets up the groups, allows the membership to be fluid but refrains from setting the agenda. It is up to the group to do so. The wise manager also permits the group to deal with issues which she personally does not approve of; the idea is to benefit from the multiplicity of perspectives and not to suppress those which we do not favour. Having people agreeing with us is not the purpose of these meetings. But in order to stimulate innovation and creativity, the manager can "disturb the field" by suggesting and presenting ambiguous challenges so that group members can confront difficult and complex issues. It is important to have an ambience where it is permissible to express oneself honestly, where people are not punished for sharing what they really think and where managers respect divergent views.

Activity 7.3

Notice the existence of self-organising groups in your work organisation. How do they emerge, how do they operate?

The "both… and…" of power

When power is focused on the few and imposed on others, we find as a result very stable organisations which are unable to deal creatively with a complex world, as they can only handle what those who hold power view as worthy of attention. In that situation, strategic ideas can only come from the top and these people need to be outstanding for the organisation to find creative ways of surviving and thriving in a complex and uncertain world. However, if power is too widely dispersed, we find a sort of anarchy where people are unable to engage in deep learning about the problems they experience and in terms of what direction the organisation needs to pursue.

In the well-functioning organisation, power is widely and unequally distributed. While the tight control of the authoritarian and top-down organisation is usually recognised as not being very useful, the anarchy which results in an organisation where "everyone has equal power" is not often acknowledged. For a work organisation to perform very well in complexity, we need both the distribution of power to all and the retention of power by those who lead the organisation. When it is appropriate to do so, leaders move into a totally democratic style but they also exercise their authority in a hierarchical manner when the situation warrants that they do so. As we have seen previously, they also hand over power to workers who operate in an autonomous manner when it fits to the context and the situation.

Activity 7.4

Reflecting on your organisation, identify how power is distributed.

– Is it highly concentrated or is it too widely distributed?
– How can the balance of power be improved?

The creative organisation

Celebration of dissent

Chaotic conditions require an organisational culture which facilitates creativity.

Too often in many projects, creativity is stifled. There are many barriers to creativity in organisations. The love of conformity is probably one of the most important obstacles. Managers with poor self-esteem often demand that others should simply comply with their wishes and some organisations also expect people to conform and surrender their individuality and creativity. Conformity does not lead to creativity. If we want innovation, we have to celebrate dissent and value those who do not agree with us.

About risk-taking and "mistakes"

A culture which values risk-taking is one which helps the creative process. If we are punished for our creative ideas, we stop producing them. As we have discussed before, re-framing how we view "mistakes" is crucial. If people are castigated for their creative ideas which turn out to be a "mistake", they will cease to be creative. Not all creative ideas will work in practice. There is always wastage in the creative process. For each creative idea which works, there will be several which will not be feasible. Some organisations ridicule or punish people whose ideas have not worked. If this is what the organisation does, workers will stop producing ingenious and imaginative ideas or they will not share their creative suggestions in the work situation.

The creative organisation values people as it is those with good self-esteem who are able to take the risks entailed when one is being creative. Good self-esteem gives the confidence for taking risks. Therefore, in such organisations, risk-taking is valued and managers lead the way by being themselves adventurous risk-takers.

Being involved

Encouraging people to respond, to take part and to stop being mere by-standers is also important. To be a non-bystander involves taking risks. The more responses we make, the more fully involved we are, the more creative we become.

Suspending judgment

Judgment is anathema to creativity in its early stages. In many organisations in middle- and low-income countries, there are high levels of negative critical judgment. At the organisational level, the use of judgment needs to be controlled. Disparaging verdicts on people's innovative ideas stifle the creative process. We do need to protect the early phases of creativity. Furthermore, the process itself must be kept separate from judgment. It is useful to set up an arena where judgment is eliminated. Creativity circles allow this to happen – in these groups, people are encouraged to be as original, inventive and ingenious as possible.

We need organisations which value absurdity. Judging is a later stage when we consider the feasibility of an idea and it must not be allowed to suppress creativity.

In some work organisations, judging and being critical of innovative ideas arise from workers being envious of their more ingenious colleagues. Envy can be a very problematic emotion in many projects and can lead to negative outcomes. We need to encourage people with a tendency towards destructive envy to emulate their colleagues, because envy when used positively is information telling us what we would like to be and to achieve.

The importance of slack time and time-out

To be innovative, we need to have slack time, i.e., time when we can take a distance from the day to day routine work of organisations and focus on different things. Great ideas tend to emerge from our quiet, reflective periods.

To develop creative ideas takes time and it is important to invest in this time. The creative process can be lengthy and we may have to wait for innovative ideas to emerge. But without that investment there will be no or little creativity.

We saw earlier, when we discussed the Gestalt cycle, that the normal healthy cycle goes through a period of quietness, of rest and of incubation. The void between cycles is also vital as new figures emerge from this void and from this in-between space. Too often in the too-busy organisation, there is no slack time at all. Creative organisations recognise how crucial it is to build in some idle time – quieter moments on a regular basis when people have an opportunity to move into an incubation period. When we are caught in over busy-ness, we are less likely to be very prolific in generating creative ideas. People also need periods in the working week when they are undisturbed. We have to protect our time if we want to be more creative. Appointments, systems and effective time-management enable us to protect our time. Time spent in engaging in non-purposeful activity, with no demand and no performance, is useful creative time. It is during these moments that we obtain creative insights and intuitive ideas. Slack time can be used for routine activities such as filing and sorting out our paperwork. Quiet time is crucial for inquiry, reflection and learning. Active, over-busy organisations have to learn to stop "doing" at regular intervals and to engage in "being".

Activity 7.5

– **Does your organisation have any slack time?**
– **What can you do to ensure that there is sufficient slack time at your workplace?**
– **Do you personally have enough quiet time on a regular basis?**

Organisational culture for promoting creativity

Believing in the organisational capacities to be creative and believing that people who work there have much potential is an important aspect of the creative organisation.

If people do not adopt this perspective, the organisation will be seized by fear and engage in unhelpful strategies as discussed in an earlier chapter.

Activity 7.6

– **What hinders creativity in your work organisation?**
– **What can you do to remove these obstacles to creativity?**

Activity 7.7

Organise a creativity group in your work setting, one where members are encouraged in generating creative ideas, in engaging in useful problem solving and in improving quality.

– **How can you organise such a group?**
– **What ground rules would help you in ensuring that the group functions well?**

Organisation analysis

As managers, we can use the following framework as a checklist to see to what extent the setting is a humane one where people are intrinsically motivated to work well.

The environment

What sort of environment is it? Is it purely functional or is it pleasing to the senses? Is it a safe one physically and psychologically? Is our soul stirred by working in this setting? To what extent is it conducive to creativity? Do people have a space to personalise the work environment? What is the general atmosphere?

We do know that people are profoundly affected by their work environment and yet it seems that very little attention is given to this by project leaders. Our environment affects our physical, emotional, mental, psychological and spiritual well-being. If we want people to thrive in our work organisations and we are concerned about both the level of contentment and the output of workers, we have to pay much attention to the context in which people work. Do we, as managers, ensure that people work in an environment which is physically, emotionally and aesthetically satisfying to our workers?

The social setting

How are workers treated? Is their humanity and their dignity attended to with respect? Do people seem to enjoy the work they do? Are there many opportunities for creative self-organising groups? Is there a sense of community and camaraderie? Is there nurturing, relaxing and challenging support? What are the means of communications? Are people satisfied with both the quality and the quantity of communication? Are people overloaded with meetings which do not concern them? Are they able to participate in decisions which concern them? Are people able to meet in an informal manner to generate ideas?

Technical support

Do people have sufficient resources to carry out their work? Is the necessary equipment available and well-maintained? Are people sufficiently trained? How is continuous education and learning managed in the organisation?

Use of time

How do people spend time? What is the balance between active and quiet times? Are there opportunities to meet socially during official work time? How effective is the time management of workers and managers? Do people value time as an important resource?

What are the working hours? Are these flexible enough to accommodate the needs of different workers as well as the needs of the task and those of the receivers of the service provided?

The nature of the work

Are the outcomes of the work worthy of the commitment of the people employed there? Are ethical and moral issues addressed?

How does the work undertaken by the organisation contribute to the community, the wider society and the universe? What is the wider ecological dimension of the project and of the work organisation?

The organisational culture

What is the culture of the organisation? In what way does the culture stifle creativity and learning? How does it facilitate creativity and learning? What are the important aspects of culture which have to change?

A celebration of conflict: the importance of freedom of expression

We saw earlier how subversive action is encouraged in the effective organisation. Conflict is important to us. Many of us have learned

that conflict is not valuable. What is not worthwhile is the type of
conflict where people get hurt because it is based on personal
attacks, on jealousies and on envy between colleagues. But conflict
over ideas in a climate of mutual respect is to be encouraged. It is
the disagreement with our ideas that lead us to review them and to
ameliorate these ideas. To have the right milieu for creative conflict
to thrive, we have to ensure that there is sufficient respect between
people; very importantly we have to safeguard freedom of expression. We cannot advance if we prevent freedom of expression.
People who are fearful of the liberty of others to express themselves
are inadequate people whose existence depends on others being
subservient to them. As leaders, ensuring our own personal development, which means that we attempt to operate mainly from an
"I'm O.K." stance, we need not fear conflict and we need not fear
to hear what others have to say. We do not necessarily have to agree
with others but we need to listen and use these opportunities to further our learning.

Eustress and distress in work organisations

In many work organisations in middle- and low-income countries,
people feel very stressed. We need to distinguish between positive
stress, also called eustress, and distress, the negative side of stress.
Eustress is what spurs us on, what energizes us and what often leads
to outstanding performance and great satisfaction. Eustress is experienced as both enjoyable and useful. Distress is not only unpleasant, it is also detrimental and damaging to both the individual and
the organisation. We do know that people's health and their productivity are adversely affected by distress. The quality of the outcome
of the task is affected when workers are distressed. However, there
are major individual differences between what is perceived as distress and what is viewed as eustress. What is eustress to one person
may be very distressing to another. The challenge for work organisations is to generate sufficient eustress for people to be fully productive without creating distress, while being aware of the varia-
tions between particular workers. An important element to prevent

distress is the feeling of control which workers have over their work. When we take note of the humanity of others, when we appreciate that there is life outside work, when we do not impose unrealistic expectations on others, when we ensure that workers are not overloaded but can exercise their talents and use their abilities and capacities fully and when workers have a say in all important issues which affect them, we promote eustress and diminish the potential harmful effect of distress.

On the importance of continuous change

A complexity perspective to work organisations means that we need to engage in a process of continuous change. What is the "truth" at a specific historical period may be found later to be inadequate and may need considerable amendment. A theme running throughout this book is that change (or learning) is a continuous process. This applies to what is said in the chapters of this book. I am sharing ideas and principles, not prescriptions. These ideas are found to be effective in many circumstances at this moment in time. But we have to keep revising these and in a few years' time, a similar book may contain very different messages, as we do not know what exactly will be helpful with the passage of time. Therefore, work organisations need to constantly engage in unlearning and learning. Change, including change in ideas and principles to guide us, is therefore a dominant theme. It is to the process of change itself that we turn in the next chapter.

References and further reading

Clarkson P. (1995) *Change in Organisations*, Whurr, London.

Clarkson P. 1993, *On Psychotherapy*, Whurr, London.

Morgan G. (1988) *Riding the Waves of Change – Developing Managerial Competencies for a Turbulent World*, Jossey Bass, San Francisco.

Senge P. (1992) *The Fifth Discipline – The Art and Practice of the Learning Organization*, Century Business, London.

Stacey R. (1992) *Managing Chaos*, Kogan Page, London.

Chapter 8   The change process

The issue

Change has been a constant theme throughout this book and as some management writers point out, the only thing about which we can be sure nowadays is change itself. Project leaders have to understand the process of change to be able to manage effectively. Profound change involves a bereavement process when we give up the old; this is often experienced as painful by many people. But if we accept this stage, which is like a sort of "mini-death", we can go on to re-construct something new. Managers have a role in helping people through the change process.

Organisation development

In the same way as in previous chapters, the importance of personal development for staff and managers has been stressed; the organisation itself has to engage in a process of development. In the previous chapter, we have looked at the characteristics of organisations which are effective in a turbulent chaotic world where complexity is the norm. Organisation development involves continuous unlearning and learning at the organisational level.

The change process

As with other models in management, many models offered to project leaders about change are framed within a linear approach. They describe the change process in terms of simple statements and steps; notably "where are we now", "where do we want to be" and "how do we get from the former to the latter"? This model sees change as evolutionary with easily identifiable steps which are clear and simple. Significant change is much more complex than that suggested by the linear model.

We can learn much from a complexity perspective to help us understand the turmoil as well as the patterns of the change process.

Complexity revisited: the future is always uncertain

As we have seen in the earlier chapters, the future is always uncertain. This does not mean that we cannot have our dreams and things which we would like to achieve. But we have to accept that no-one can tell us in advance what the outcome of a change process will be and, generally, strategies emerge as we go along. In other words, when we are engaged in a change process we have an idea of what we would like, but this idea evolves as we embark on our journey, the aims and goals become redefined and keep arising from new elements along the course of the journey. Therefore we discover where we are going along the way while we are involved in the process. Strategies are not predetermined, they emerge.

A crucial message therefore is that we do not know in advance what will be the exact result of a change process. The future is unknown and unknowable but we influence that future. As change agents, we have to accept that we do not know what the consequences of what we undertake will actually be – especially long-term ones – as we cannot predict the consequences of even very small factors. The outcome of a change process may be in our favour or it may be to our detriment. We may be able to foresee some of the consequences but we cannot anticipate the full implications.

This primary health-care project was set up twenty years ago with the aims of improving child health through immunisation programmes and of reducing the birth rate through a family planning programme. A long-term effect of the project has been that of giving women a new role. Local women have become very assertive. The project leader is used to clients who passively do as they are told and does not know how to deal with users who demand, argue, complain and want an active role in health matters.

Activity 8.1

Think about a change process which you have undertaken some time in the past.

– **What were the long-term outcomes? Did you predict these at the outset?**
– **Have the long-term outcomes proved to be advantageous or problematic?**

Change occurs in far-from-equilibrium conditions

Organisations operating in an ossified or disintegrated state are not open to change. They are rigid, stable and refuse to acknowledge internal and external factors which affect them. Stability is the enemy of change. To be open to change, organisations (and individuals) have to be in a state far-from-equilibrium, which is also potentially very creative.

About fractals: the part contains the whole

Fractal is the term used for every tiny part of a system and complexity demonstrates that each fractal of a system contains the patterns of the whole system. Using this analogy for thinking about organisations leads us to view each part of the system as carrying the characteristics of the wider system. In a way each fractal contains the whole system. When we consider change, this means that an intervention in one small part of the system will have an effect, at some level, on the whole of the system.

In this international NGO, there is a team whose brief is to monitor gender issues both at the level of the organisation and at the level of the projects which it implements. As part of their documenting of factors hindering women's progress in the workplace, this team uncovers the high levels of stress for women in the organisation. It decides to put stress on its own agenda. In a matter of months, the whole organisation is looking at stress as an issue for workers, both male and female, either directly as a result of this small team's work, or indirectly or somehow as if by chance.

Activity 8.2

Reflect on your own particular project, section or department. To what extent do you find characteristics of the larger organisation in your particular section?

Small interventions lead to important results: the butterfly effect

As we have seen earlier, positive feedback in complex systems may lead to totally unexpected outcomes, especially in the long term, the so-called butterfly-wing effect. In work organisations, small interventions may lead to quite large, at times totally unpredictable outcomes. A minimal event may intensify, causing substantial changes in the whole system.

Important points about the butterfly-wing effect are that this escalation from something very small to a large and consequential outcome usually takes time, and the links between cause and effect disappear as the relationships become very complex. It also means that an extremely small intervention can have a large effect, but we do not know what the long-term outcomes will be. The reverse of this suggests that large interventions tend to lead to relatively small and negligible results. For example, one person working differently, at some level, will cause a turbulence in the wider system. It is not the norm for one person to change a huge system by him/herself; however, there will be a disturbance, but whether the consequence will be advantageous or not cannot be known in advance.

This is a community where women are very oppressed, reflecting the position of women in the wider society. The project leader is aware of the sensitivity of gender issues and that to address these directly will be very detrimental to the project. Her only intervention is to facilitate women meeting together and encouraging them to share their experiences. Over a period of five years, many outcomes have resulted from this minimal intervention. The women have discussed several important issues: family planning, the education of girls, the importance of valuing daughters and the worthwhile contributions of girls and women to the community. They have become very empowered and have undertaken several concrete projects. For the first time, they are also very aware of their position in the society and want to find ways of improving the lot of women. The project leader has been careful not to impose her views; all she seems to do is to sit around and encourage them to talk. The concrete outcomes have simply emerged. But these are not welcomed by all in the community. There is now antagonism between some men and some women in the community. The project leader is confident that the community will find its own creative ways of dealing with this conflict, but she is also aware that she cannot be totally certain that this is what will happen. There are other possible outcomes; for example, the men with power in the community could become even more repressive and authoritarian.

Valuable organisational change: continuous learning

To engage in continuous organisational development, unlearning and learning along the way, it is useful for an organisation to operate from the far-from-equilibrium condition at the edge of chaos. This state is propitious for creativity, where we have bounded instability with people being both pro-active and reactive, embracing turbulence and chaos instead of retreating into unhelpful strategies to protect themselves against anxiety.

Organisational change to be avoided: moving towards stability

The linear paradigm sees organisational change as a means of fixing problems within the organisation in order to reach a level of "normality", i.e., a state of equilibrium. The belief is that there is a perfect state towards which an organisation can move; from the stability of this flawless state, the organisation will be able to be more productive and effective. Those who are concerned about the human factor in organisations, add that the work organisation will also be

more humane towards its workers. This stable, non-conflictual setting where all is well, is what many project leaders aspire to. I hope
that the notion that this is not so has been gained from the previous
chapters. This "paradise" does not exist and will never exist. In
addition, the aim of organisational change is not to move towards
this utopia which is just that: a figment of our imagination, a piece
of fantasy which we fabricate, possibly as a means of helping us
with the anxiety which living in a chaotic world arouses in us.
Organisational change, from a complexity perspective, is that of
establishing the conditions which facilitate the organisation's being
engaged in continuous learning, in order to ensure that the organisation is in a state of perpetual metamorphosis, constantly self-
renewing and concerned with continual transformation.

We have already seen the value of having sufficient creative tension
through the process of spontaneous self-organising and through an
acceptance of constructive conflict within the organisation. We note
the emphasis on processes or means of incessantly initiating novelty
and transmutation. From this paradigm, there is a switch from stress-
ing the importance of outcomes – which linear models emphasise – to
that of focusing on processes. Crucial roles for the manager include
becoming aware of the importance of processes, helping to eliminate
the barriers to continuous change and facilitating the organisation's
giving up its unhelpful stratagems which stop it from developing.

Mental flexibility

Organisational development therefore includes the ability to be
aware of the paradigm within which one is at present operating, i.e.,
the dominant paradigm present in the organisation. More importantly, it demands being aware of how one is creating this paradigm
and how the organisation creates its own realities. For each new paradigm can eventually become a prison, or another way of stifling
new learning unless we develop the awareness of how we construct
our perspectives on the world.

Change "management": discovery

In the linear model of change, change management consists of deciding in advance what change should be instituted and taking well-defined steps to reach this desired outcome with an emphasis on control. From a complexity perspective, dealing with change is about discovery. It is engaging in a process where we patiently wait for something to emerge and take shape. It is not about achieving a predetermined outcome. It is something which materialises from spontaneous self-organising groups. This does not mean, as has been pointed out before, that we do not have our dreams or that we do not know where we would like to be in the future. We have ideas about what we would like and about what we want to achieve and intentions about the means of accomplishing our goals. However, paradoxically, it is about having dreams and letting go at the same time. By letting go, we are not forcing the issue, we allow our dreams to change along the way. More importantly, we accept that although we may know where we would like to go, we do not know how we are going to get there – the road which leads us there will probably be full of surprises and we will discover along the way how to deal with the good and the bad. We will discover the solutions and where we are going during the "odyssey" – during the journey we undertake. It is a real voyage of discovery, full of possibilities.

The effective manager therefore accepts that any "plan" may be troubled by the unanticipated and the unforeseen. This style of managing involves learning how to deal with fluctuations and finding creative means of going with the flow. Change is not managed in the sense of control. Through the ordinary conversations of people, each one of them with their own intentions, strategies for change emerge.

Activity 8.3

– **How does your work organisation handle change?**
– **Do people have utopian ideals of a perfect state which they ought to reach?**
– **How flexible is the organisation?**

About endings and beginnings

Starting something new usually means first ending and mourning for the old and for what has been. We experience this when we buy a new car or a new pair of shoes or move house. However much we want this new object, we surprise ourselves by feeling sad for the battered car, the cramped house or the worn pair of shoes. The first step towards making an important beginning is therefore to make an ending. Endings contain the seeds for new beginnings.

Daphne has just been offered a management post in a newly created department at the Ministry of Health. This means that she will have to move from the small town in which she lives to the city. This is an important promotion for her. It confirms that she is a capable worker and the new post will probably lead to better career opportunities. Her new house, subsidised by her employers, will be much larger than the one in which she now lives. She is very excited by the prospect of this new post. Yet, she feels depressed and does not understand why this should be so. She has so much wanted this to happen; it is a dream come true for her and she feels so sad.

Tim works for an international NGO and his 5-year project has now come to an end. Funding is definitely not being renewed but the major activities of the project will continue, financed and staffed locally. This is a real ending as far as the international NGO is concerned. Personally, Tim is sad about leaving but at the same time, he is looking forward to being back home, seeing his friends and family and furthering his career. In the last few weeks, he has met with many local people to discuss with them how they would like to handle the project after he is gone. It is obvious that the project will be much altered but Tim realises that this has to be so, and the local villagers have been very innovative with their ideas about how to sustain this health initiative. This will indeed be a new beginning for the local community.

Jeremiah has worked for disability projects in this area for over thirty years. Funding has been drastically cut back and there is no choice but to make some staff redundant. It is felt that the kindest way of doing so is to offer early retirement to those who are aged 50 and over. His work has been the centre and focus of Jeremiah's life. When he was given the news, he felt totally lost and in a state of despair. The leaving party given in his honour was very moving. He remained very depressed and the early weeks have been very difficult. He has felt very let down and, at times, has been very angry about what has happened to him. He felt that he did not deserve this as a "reward" for his commitment and his hard work. But in the last few days, he has noticed that his view is starting to change. It is good not to have to get up so early every morning and he can now do as he pleases. He is thinking of starting a vegetable patch in his garden. Maybe, some of the disabled youngsters he knows would like to help. He will go to the market to find out what seeds he can sow at this time of the year and he will call at the youth club on his way back.

Endings: grieving and bereavement

The bereavement process which we undergo when someone dies is apparent whenever there is a sense of loss. In any consequential change, there is loss and the bereavement cycle can be observed. The example of Jeremiah above, is an illustration of this cycle. At the beginning, there is often a state of shock in people; disbelief about what is happening is quite common. After the state of shock, anger surfaces; people become angry about the change which is taking place. Then follows a time of depression when despair, loss of energy, despondency and discouragement are experienced. Sometimes, depression precedes anger. During that time, people ask themselves why this change should be happening to them; the "why us" questions abound. It is generally only after this phase that people can go on to face the change. At this stage, they move out of relative passivity and can become actively involved in the change process with the questions now focusing around "what can we do?" Eventually people adapt to the change. Life being cyclical, another change will inevitably occur with the same process reappearing once again. In the normal course of a change process, people complete the cycle. The time period varies according to the severity or otherwise of the change. If a change process is minimal, we may experience this cycle only slightly and over a very short period of time. When the change is deep and profound, it may take us a very long time to complete the cycle. Sometimes people and organisations do not complete the cycle and remain fixed at some stages, maybe those of anger or depression.

Like Jeremiah, Grace has been made redundant. She also loved her work and feels very angry that she has been forced to retire. She thought that she would be working for at least another ten years. She has never considered retirement and does not know what to do with herself. Her children are now grown up and have left home. They have moved to the city where they work, so she now sees them only for a few days a year. She is becoming bitter about her early retirement. It is all the fault of this young manager, Anita, who has only joined the organ-isation two years ago. Grace has decided that Anita is one of these hard career women who do not care about anyone. They are much worse than men. Grace spends much of her time gossiping about her ex-colleagues, especially about Anita. She has revealed to her friends many things which she observed while she was still employed. Recently, she has been keeping an eye on what goes on with Anita's children. Her gossip now includes the bad behaviour of these children; of course, they would turn out like this with such a mother who does not really care for them. And is it true that Anita's husband was heard shouting and leaving abruptly in his car yesterday?

Helping people deal with loss: an important role for dealing with change

An important function for project leaders dealing with a change process is that of assisting people to come to terms with the change, and supporting their grief for what is being left or what is lost.

Managers dealing with change are usually advised to communicate assiduously. This is very good counsel but what the advice ignores is that, in the early stage, while people are in a state of shock and may be denying what is really happening, they simply do not hear us. People in shock hear very little of what is said or if they do, they cannot assim-ilate the information at this time. Especially when people do not want to face reality, they may not hear what we are saying. We have to take this into account in our communications and we have to allow for that fact. We may have to repeat ourselves many times for the message to be heard.

Emotions at work: allowing emotions to surface

As we have seen, grief, depression and anger are common emotions in the early days of an important change process. The caring and effective manager not only allows these emotions to surface, but enables people to deal with them adequately.

Emotions are often denied a place in work situations. We cannot stop ourselves feeling strong emotions simply because we are at work. To deny them does not help anyone, least of all the organisation in the long run. As managers, we have a role to play in giving emotions a place in work situations. We also have to accept the legitimacy of emotions and not see them as bad things. There is nothing wrong about emotions as these are data containing useful information for us. It is what we choose to do as a result of feeling certain emotions which may be considered harmful. The expression of emotions is to be encouraged but, of course, in helpful and constructive ways. The simplest way is to give people an opportunity to talk about their feelings and just to listen. When they do so, it is crucial that we accept the authenticity and validity of what they are feeling, even if we do not agree with them. Too often, when managers allow and encourage the verbalisation of people's feelings, they then proceed to put people down by denying the legitimacy of these emotions. Managers often do so inadvertently by saying such things as "there is no need for you to feel this way…" and the effect is to disavow the pertinence and validity of what people are experiencing. What they do need from us is sufficient empathy, but we have to acknowledge that even the most compassionate person cannot fully understand someone else's feelings. We have to be humble with our empathy, recognising that we do not know what the other person is actually experiencing. When we encourage the articulation of anger, we have to tolerate anger being focused on us. This does not mean that we accept responsibility and blame for what is outside our jurisdiction, but that we understand that other people may perceive us as the perpetrator of their misfortunes. We do need to protect ourselves emotionally and our own self-care is crucial.

Emotions such as anger provide us with much energy, including energy for action; it is useful to re-direct the energy discharge to accomplish something productive.

When people are at the emotional stage of the bereavement cycle, we have to remember that they tend to be re-active and simply respond to what comes their way. When emotions have not been expressed, the assimilation of information may still be impaired, as people are blinded by the force of their feelings. Therefore, once again we have to be aware that, although we may have attempted to communicate, others may not have heard us. Afterwards, as long as the cycle is being completed, people become pro-active. They are able to find out what it is that they can do to deal with whatever change is facing them. They can now take note of what is being said and can find creative responses to what is confronting them.

Of course, like all models, the bereavement cycle is not as simple and orderly as what I have presented. In real life, things are much more complex and disorderly. The bereavement cycle is the pattern which we can often observe in a profound change period, a pattern in the complexity of the real world where the expression of this cycle takes many different forms.

It has been decided at regional level that primary health-care teams in the region are to be re-structured. As multi-disciplinary work is seen as important, teams of health personnel – nurses, midwives and doctors – will work alongside teachers, health educators, social workers and water and sanitation workers. Robert, the doctor, who up to now has been in charge of medical personnel, believes that this is a good thing – a view not shared by his staff. He is keen to persuade his staff that this is a positive move. He has attended management courses where it was pointed out that in times of change, he needs to communicate as he has never done before. He conscientiously holds regular staff meetings to inform his staff of what to expect and of the time-table of the changes. These meetings have been very stormy with angry exchanges between Robert and the nurses. They are accusing him of a number of things. At times, these are very personal attacks. Robert does not like displays of emotions and he uses his position as chairperson of these meetings to move people quickly through the different items. Meetings ought to end on time – something else which he learned at his management course and he is determined to do so. He keeps himself very busy attending many meetings with the local Authority and Water and Sanitation staff about to join them. He also has to travel to the Regional Headquarters quite often. He is very good at feeding back information to his own staff. Recently, his secretary pointed out to him that members of his staff are complaining about not seeing much of him. Robert is vaguely aware that he prefers to be attending these outside meetings. The health centre used to have a very cosy and friendly atmosphere. Nowadays, it is not very pleasant. There is much gossip and people are starting to complain about many minor issues. Staff meetings have become unbearable. Robert cannot understand what is going on: the proposed change is for the benefit of the users and his staff used to be so concerned about quality of service to users.

Sally is the project leader for a community-based rehabilitation service for disabled children providing support for parents. She is herself a physiotherapist and has led a small team of occupational therapists, other physiotherapists, social workers and a speech therapist. It has been decided that their services should become an integral part of the primary health-care services in the area which is managed by a medical practitioner. Sally will act only as coordinator as the medical practitioner will be responsible for the whole team, including the present health service team of medical assistants and nurses. Her staff are very unhappy about the proposed change. They could hardly believe what she announced to them a month ago when she came back after having been asked to attend a planning meeting at the Regional Headquarters. Sally has patiently been replying to the many questions which they keep asking her. She is aware that she has already given them much of this information at the regular staff meetings which they hold. But they do not appear to be processing this information. She is very busy as there are so many meetings to attend with the Health Services team and she has to travel to the Regional Headquarters every fortnight. But she has decided to abandon other work at present and to spend much of her time simply being available to staff. She ensures that she is free during official coffee times. She has noticed that since the news has been announced, staff tend to congregate in the kitchen at other times during the day. As much as possible, Sally drops in, makes herself yet another cup of coffee, and chats casually, answering as well as she is able the questions which inevitably come her way. The two occupational therapists, who were always so full of energy, appear despondent much of the time and Jenny, the speech therapist, is starting to be very aggressive towards Sally.

The changes are due to take place next month and much remains to be sorted out. Unfortunately, her team appears unable to contribute to constructive ideas for her to take back to the Regional Headquarter. This is not at all like them; they are usually very creative people.

Sally has decided to do some reading about the change process. She is very busy but must find some time for reading. She has bought this book recommended by a Management Consultant friend who also mentioned something about the grieving process.

Sally has just been able to skim-read the book where they talk about the bereavement cycle. It all now makes sense to her. She has announced to her staff that they will spend a whole day on a workshop to discuss the change at the end of the month. They are busy and clinics will have to be cancelled but she has already discussed the need for her team to annul these clinics with the disabled and parents' representatives.

She plans to spend the whole day in an ending workshop, helping her staff to end and celebrate the time they have been together as a small team. After this, she will see whether they are ready to prepare for the future.

Like Sally, in the example given above, managers can encourage people to do their grieving for what has been, so that they can move on. We cannot connect with the new until we have said good-bye to the past. If we decide to hold an "endings" workshop, our aim would be to encourage people to complete the later stages of the Gestalt cycle – satisfaction and withdrawal. It is giving people an opportunity to complete anything which is unfinished so that they are ready to start a new cycle. We give people time for reflection, encouraging them to consider what learning has taken place and the significance of this learning for the future. It is therefore a time for contemplation before we let go of what has been, so that we can move on and start another cycle.

Activity 8.4

Ideas for an endings workshop:
In an endings workshop, encourage people to express their feelings and their emotions about what they are leaving. It is important to enable the expression of both positive and negative emotions.
People need an opportunity to verbalise the following:

- **Anger: what are they/others angry about**
- **Guilt: what they wished they had done/not done, what they feel they ought to have done/not done**
- **Regret: what they regret having done/not done**
- **Pain/hurt: what do they feel pain about, what are their hurts?**
- **Loss: what are they grieving about now?**

Invite them to say what they have liked, appreciated, what has been helpful, what were their joys.
Then they need a time of reflection on whatever learning has taken place:

- **What are they dissatisfied with? What, if anything, would they do differently next time?**
- **What are they satisfied with? What have they achieved?**
- **What have been the good things, the happy times and memories?**

Celebration of time spent together: whatever the level of satisfaction or dissatisfaction, it is important to celebrate the time that people have spent together, the interrelationships that have been formed and which, at some level, they will keep for the rest of their lives. Different societies have various rituals and it is useful to draw on whatever is appropriate at the local level. Rituals such as singing, dancing, sharing food and drink together are all valuable. After this "looking back" stage, we assist the transitional stage between the past and the future. We give them an opportunity to move into the new. Expression of relief about the past provides this

movement. We encourage them to express relief about what they no longer have to do/not do.

Looking into the future, it is important to facilitate the expression of fear and anxiety which may impede the motion into the future. We invite them to tell us what they fear about the new/ the future. We can end on a positive note asking them to express what they are looking forward to in the new/future.

A note on survivors' guilt

When an ending is being processed because people have been made redundant, we need to acknowledge the difficulties for people who stay in the organisation, those who have not lost their jobs. We know that survivors in times of "disaster" feel guilty for having survived. We also know that those who stay on when others have been made redundant suffer from this survivor's guilt. Therefore, we have to acknowledge the distress not only of those who are leaving but also of those who stay behind. It is useful to give them a voice to say what they are feeling.

Activity 8.5

Focus on an important change in your life.

– **Did you go through a bereavement process?**
– **How was it handled by those around you?**
– **How did you deal with it?**
– **Was there anything which could have been done in a better way?**
– **What lessons have you learned from this process?**

First- and second-level change

In organisational work, we differentiate between first- and second-level change. In first-level change, there appears to have been change, but, in effect, nothing has been altered fundamentally: perspectives, beliefs, attitudes and the deeper levels remain the same.

In first-level change, the saying "the more it changes, the more it remains the same" applies. In second-level change, something fundamentally changes: the individual, the group and the organisation will never be the same again. The deep-level beliefs, attitudes, assumptions and the paradigms within which people operate have changed. This sort of change can be an evolutionary step, happening as a process of growth, or it can be quite dramatic and unprecedented in style.

Unhelpful change

Not all change processes are helpful to us, and sometimes we find that there has been no change at all; all we have is a tinkering with superficial issues disguised as change. In spite of many alterations, there may have been no change at all or very little (first-level change) and sometimes change can be destructive to individuals and to organisations. For example, an organisation may appear to go through a process of change but its world view and its perspectives remain the same. People in the organisation usually react cynically to whatever change process is in motion as they recognise that these have been undertaken before.

This Health Authority is having yet another re-structuring with many departments being reorganised. In the last 15 years, there have been four of these major re-structurings with some minor ones occasionally. The service which users receive has remained very much the same during that time. Staff are getting ready for another period of not knowing exactly what will happen, waiting for the new appointments to be made, not being sure who the next boss will be and what it means for them. The details will be announced in the next few weeks and the changes will be implemented soon afterwards. At present, many managers are being interviewed for the proposed new posts. They feel very stressed as they do not know whether they will have a managerial function in the new structure or whether they will revert back to a mainly technical position. People are finding it difficult to concentrate on the task of providing a service to users. Members of staff are very cynical

*about the proposed change. They have seen it all before. It is as if,
when the organisation reaches a certain point, it cannot help going
backwards and starting the same motions all over again. Staff sarcas-
tically suggest that this occurs whenever the organisation becomes
really effective.*

Sometimes organisations simply attempt what is humanly impossible.
Often there is a wish to be perfect. In an imperfect world, there is
bound to be disappointment.

*This NGO believes that it is crucial for them to provide the best to their
users. They have commissioned a number of surveys to find out what
users living in a very deprived area would like. The list is a formidable one, as the community perceives the NGO as their saviour, able to
provide almost anything. The NGO has altered many of its services
and the way they function. Most importantly, they have engaged in a
"culture" change for staff, urging staff to devote their time to serving
these communities. This has not been accompanied by any increase in
the number of staff or by any strategies to support people who already
feel overloaded and overstretched. People are very committed and they
are working even harder. Yet there is much unhappiness around. People
are feeling even more stressed and many are becoming very disillusioned.*

Common occurrences with second level change

Clarkson (1993) describes some very common characteristics of second-level change. There are often very strong emotions surrounding
the change, an intensity of both feelings and energy. These strong
emotions usually include the despair of the void, the notion that
things have to get much worse before they can get better and the
descent into what mystical people have called the "dark night of the
soul". In real transformation, this phase is a very common one. Most
people find it very difficult to live in that phase and to survive and
come out of it creatively. It is crucial to believe that this is potentially fertile ground from which a new and rich pattern will sooner

or later emerge. It is this conviction which keeps us going when we are feeling at our lowest and enables the fruitfulness of this void to develop.

Letting go

For those who love control, letting go is an almost impossible suggestion. As we have seen in an earlier chapter, when we are in the void, when we are in the abyss and we feel despair, the most useful strategy is to let go, to stop wishing or attempting to control and to trust that sooner or later, the figure will emerge from this barren, empty space.

Giving up our old beliefs, our old ways of dealing with the world and our outmoded and obsolete paradigm is important to allow a new one to evolve and to emerge. We need to empty what is in the vessel for it to be filled again.

The void revisited

Most traditional societies have ways of dealing with this space. In modern societies, we have become very uncomfortable with the void and we attempt to bypass it. If instead of avoidance, we learn to accept and to face this space, we often encounter a transformation. When we are in the void, it is useful to do one thing at a time, to know that the discomfort when there is no clear figure will not last forever, to trust that sooner or later we will be guided by our intuition and very importantly, to accept that the "bad" is part and parcel of life.

In second level change, the void is a good space to be in. Even if we feel uncomfortable in the void, acceptance of its importance and learning to let go are useful strategies as we wait for a figure to emerge. This is the space between the old cycle and the new one. As many writers have pointed out, creativity and second-level change happen in the spaces in between. When we have undergone a second-level transformation, there is often a sense of calling and the urge to convert others to our new way of thinking and to our new paradigm.

Activity 8.6

Reflect on an important change process in your personal or your work life.

– **Did you experience the void?**
– **What emotions did you feel?**
– **What behaviour did you display?**
– **How good are you at letting go?**

The role of the "community" in change

In traditional societies, the wider community had a role to play in initiation and transformation rites, notably that of welcoming back the person undergoing change as the new member, and of accepting him/her. In work organisations also, we need this welcome and this acceptance from the wider setting. If this does not occur, we find it much more difficult to implement what we have learned. Hence, the importance of developing a community spirit in work organisations.

Further reading:

Clarkson P. (1995) *Change in Organisations*, Whurr, London.

Clarkson P. (1993) *On Psychotherapy*, Jason Aronson, London.

Morgan G. (1988) *Riding the Waves of Change – Developing Managerial Competencies for a Turbulent World*, Jossey Bass, San Francisco.

Stacey R (ed.) (1993) *Strategic Thinking and the Management of Change – International Perspectives on Organisational Dynamics*, Kogan Page, London.

Watzlawick P., Weakland J. and Fisch R. (1974) *Change, Principles of Problem Formation and Problem Resolution*, Norton, London.

Chapter 9   Change agent skills

The issue

In a chaotic context where organisations, individuals and groups
have to continuously unlearn and learn, managers and project leaders become change agents, facilitating the change process both at
the individual and at the organisational level. Engaging in continuous change has been described as the positive and creative way of
dealing with the stresses of life and of work. In our world, at this
moment in its history, there are many of these life's stresses. As was
suggested earlier, to be a change agent or to be a culture worker is
a worthwhile undertaking. The effective change agent facilitates the
process for those around her. But in so doing she also encourages
people to connect with the wider society and with the universe.
Work organisations do not exist in isolation. We are all interrelated.
The change agent requires some specific skills and needs to be a
process-oriented worker. In a situation where we cannot know in
advance the outcomes of any change, we have to focus on processes. Managing projects becomes managing a process.

What it means to be a change agent

When we invite people to change, we are inviting them to come
with us to the edge of chaos. We are entreating them to leave the
safety of the known and the safety of stability to move into the
unknown, the uncertain and the unstable. Therefore it is not surprising that sometimes they refuse to accompany us, especially if
they cannot see any reason to change.

Fear as a hindrance to change

Once again we meet fear as an important obstacle to useful and productive transformation. It is often fear which provokes people to

remain set in their own rigidities: fear of the unknown, fear of the unpredictable and fear of ambiguity. To be able to engage others in a change process, we have to encourage them to confront their fear so that they can discover their own potential. The aim is to change the negative dimension of fear into its positive form: excitement. The idea is to invite people to accompany us on an adventure, to meet challenges head on, to discover new opportunities and in so doing to unearth our own creative abilities.

The facilitator's role is that of bringing the fear into the open and to encourage people to face it. It is by so doing that we discover our talents and our abilities. We are then able to turn fear into enthusiasm which provides the energy we require to accomplish whatever we have in mind.

Activity 9.1

This little exercise is useful any time we experience a paralysing type of fear.
Using some coloured crayons or pencils, draw your fear on a piece of paper. Look at what you have drawn.

– **What does it look like?**
– **What is it telling you?**
– **How can you deal with it?**
– **More importantly how can it help you?**

The change agent needs to persevere. This does not mean that we badger people into doing what we want or persist when they clearly do not want us to urge them on. To do so would be very counter-productive. But it does mean that we do not simply give up when we meet some opposition. It involves being there as a support and in an encouraging role, waiting for others to come with us to the edge of chaos, if they so choose. It means urging others to join us in facing fear so that creativity can emerge.

The importance of relationship

The change agent's most important role is to be in a relationship with the people with whom she is working. Change occurs when there is this deep relationship between people – one based on respect, esteem and trust. A crucial role therefore is that of establishing a meaningful relationship with others. Listening attentively to others, engaging in profound conversations and reflecting back what we observe in a non-judgmental manner are all important interventions.

"Disturbing the field"

When systems are operating within a stable framework, either in a state of disintegration or in a state of ossification, we have to "disturb the field" as change agents. It is by creating a disturbance that we stimulate the system towards a state "far-from-equilibrium" where it can find a creative response to its present issues. An important function of the change agent is, therefore, that of creating this disruption. It involves, in the language of Gestalt, a figure/ground reversal – we encourage the system to consider what was ground for them and invite them to see a new figure.

This project in a disadvantaged area in Africa is floundering. People in the organisation work extremely hard. The key workers are the coordinators, who manage locally trained people from the community. These coordinators are totally devoted to the project. In so doing, they neglect themselves and their families. They are all physically and emotionally exhausted. Their work is suffering and at times they are very disillusioned, although they keep on working arduously. The project leader has asked an external consultant to help the coordinators. The consultant encourages them to think of themselves as women and to review their personal goals. This is a new dimension for these women; they are not used to thinking about themselves. Their whole lives have been devoted to the service of others. By getting them to focus on themselves, the consultant disturbs their field and what was ground for them becomes a new figure.

The above example illustrates that in disturbing the field, we do not necessarily have to be provocative. We can provoke people without disturbing the field. The main skill here is to encourage others to focus on an aspect which they have so far ignored or not dealt with adequately. We need to perturb the current way of thinking without alienating people so much that we lose our relationship with them and thus are unable to continue having productive conversations with them.

Activity 9.2

Think about a change you would like to undertake in your project. Work out how you can "disturb the field" without frightening people so much that they refuse to follow you.

On risk-taking

"Dervishes gamble everything. They lose, and win the other…"

Rumi (1991) *One-handed Basket weaving – Poems on the Theme of Work*, Version by Coleman Barks, Maypop, Athens, Georgia, p. 122

The change agent is a risk-taker. As we have said before, in change we are dealing with the unknown and with the unpredictable. It is a step into the unknown, a step into the empty space.

Whatever we do entails risks. We never know whether what we propose is going to work. We have to accept this uncertainty. If we play safe and do not take risks, nothing much will happen. Engaging in a process of change is a type of gambling. As with gambling, the higher the stakes, the higher the return. Low risks tend to have low returns, while high risks have high returns. To be a good change agent, one has to learn to live dangerously and accept risk-taking.

Activity 9.3

Assess your skills as a risk-taker.

– How often are you prepared to take risks?

– What prevents you from doing so?

Inviting others to the edge of chaos

When we invite others to join us in taking a risk or in a journey of adventure, not everyone will want to join us. When we disturb the field and entreat people to take risks, many become very frightened. In groups, we often find at this stage the defence mechanisms which were described previously: fight/flight, pairing and dependency. The temptation for many managers when this happens is to make people feel safe. We intervene so that they will feel better, we make the situation less threatening and we take responsibility away from them to make them feel secure. If people are much too frightened, we may need to carry them for a short while, but if we overdo this, we create total safety again and change cannot take place. The strong urge to make things safe for people occurs because we also take in some of their anxiety and by making it safe for them we allay our own anxieties. But deep change can only take place if there is sufficient disruption of previous set patterns. As we have seen throughout this book, uncertainty, complexity and change induce anxiety. As change agents, we have to learn to live with it and encourage people to tolerate and stay with their anxiety. Sometimes this involves not rescuing them from their distress so that they are able to draw on their own inner strengths and become their own "father", as discussed in the chapter on mentoring. But of course, people will only agree to stay with us through the turbulent times, when previous paradigms are being deconstructed, if they trust us and if we have a good relationship with them. Hence, our relationship with them is the most critical element.

Helping people through the void

Anxiety occurs because in the void, there is no clear form, no clear figure. Human beings have a propensity for preferring obvious and distinct figures and patterns. This is the safety of the known. In the void, nothing is distinct. Sometimes we are totally lost because of the lack of clarity and the lack of order. It is important to help people recognise what is happening and to point out to them that if they are patient, a complete and orderly pattern will eventually materialise. As we have seen earlier, order comes out of disorder – with the reverse being also true. The change agent has to be content with living and working in the void. An important function is to enable others to stay in the void and to encourage them to view it as a potentially highly creative space to be in. The acceptance of the chaos of the void is crucial. Rather than waste energy in completing unclear figures before it is appropriate to do so, it is better for us to relocate our energy elsewhere. This is the time to do routine tasks which do not demand much thinking: clerical and administrative tasks, filing, clearing up desks and files, dealing with our mail, etc. Time is also usefully spent improving our relationships with others, reading topics which interest us, etc. Patience in the void and redirecting energy elsewhere inevitably bring rewards as issues start to emerge more clearly. The change agent's role is to assist others in coping with the emptiness and the formlessness of the void and to give them the skills they require to do so. Simply sharing our own experience of living through the void with others helps to reassure them that what they are experiencing is not only normal, but is also a very useful place to be in – a space where we are able to release our creative abilities and are capable of engaging in new learning. As we stay in that space and engage in conversations with each other, potentially creative self-organisation with emerging new forms is likely to occur.

Activity 9.4

How can you help your fellow workers through the void?

Finding out the stories

Organisations have stories. They have their own myths, dramas and legends. These are very powerful; in a subconscious way they determine what goes on in an organisation. The manager wanting to understand the deep level of an organisation, its culture and its belief systems needs to find out the stories which dominate. When we discover what they are, we can encourage people to change by altering their stories and adopting new ones. But the change agent has first to uncover these stories.

We detect stories by noticing what goes on, not only what is said but more importantly what is not said. To find stories, we find the secrets, the taboos of the organisation; we listen to the anecdotes that are recounted in staff meetings, in the corridors, at coffee time. We notice what people's perspectives of a good or bad day is; what to them is the meaning of success, failure, what is rewarded, what is punished, what their myths are about their leaders. Is there evidence of scapegoating, do people gossip, and what/who do they gossip about? What are the anomalies, the conflicts and the contradictions in the organisation?

When the story is revealed, the change agent attempts to discover the purpose of the organisation in creating these myths and these story lines, the aim being to unearth the function of these in the organisation.

An important, yet subtle, intervention is simply to reflect their current stories to people in the organisation and to encourage them to think about these stories. After confronting the present ones, they may choose to embrace new ones.

The organisation is a training school for disability workers in the developing world. Course participants come from a number of neighbouring countries. The dominant story is one of victims and persecutors. Depending on people's position in the organisation, they have different tales to tell, but the drama has a common pattern. This consists of individuals/groups feeling that they are being victimised. For example, secretaries complain non-stop about their managers. At coffee time, when the managers are absent, the anecdotes are about managers not understanding the secretaries. At staff meetings, teaching staff complain about their head of department or better still about the head of the organisation. The head of department usually criticizes the head of the organisation. Individuals and groups see themselves as the victim of someone else and whenever they are able to do so, they, in turn, become the persecutors of those whom they believe to be their persecutors. The strange thing is that every year each new group of students also follows the same pattern. In their meetings with staff, stu-

dents become very aggressive and point out all the negative points. They believe that their rights are being denied and overlook the many positive things which happen at the training school. The behaviours common in the organisation are those of blame, despair, gossip, sabotage, powerlessness, scapegoating and helplessness when in the role of victim. When in the role of persecutor, the behaviours include aggression, destructive conflict, personal attacks, non-cooperation and bullying. The story line is one of victims and persecutors with fights played in a win/lose approach. The stories serve as a defence mechanism against uncertainty. There is much uncertainty about the future in this training school. The most important uncertainty concerns the continuing existence of the training school. Funders for courses have recently been gradually cutting back on expenditure. Students depend on this outside funding as very few of them could afford the fees. Students want to come to train there, as the school has a good reputation and the certificates it issues are very much valued, but there is doubt about the future as funders have indicated that training is no longer one of their priorities. The uncertainty around the existence of the school and about whether or not there will be employment for staff are issues which the staff find too threatening to face. There are other uncertainties but the financial aspect is the major one.

Changing the stories: how to be a culture worker

We saw, in the previous chapter, the importance of culture for organisations and we talked of dynamic, empowering managers as culture workers. The best way of becoming a culture worker and of facilitating a project to adopt a more supportive and energising culture is to work with the stories. We can encourage people to change their stories. One way of doing this is to start with one's own story. If we are working as internal change agents (see fractals in the previous chapter) we are also part of the system. What this means is that we have probably inadvertently adopted the story line of the organisation, because stories are very powerful. Therefore, to change the organisational story, we need first and foremost to change our own story in the organisation. As we saw earlier, from the butterfly-effect syndrome we do know that one person acting differently in a system, at some level, influences the system. However, as we also discussed earlier, we do not know in advance the outcome of the change process.

If we have a recognised role as a change agent, we can encourage the organisation to change its story. As managers and project leaders, we can organise workshops and/or create conversations amongst people to look at the culture of the organisation and to consider to what extent the dominant stories hinder or facilitate good work. A powerful way of doing so is to use traditional stories, collage, drawings, symbols and metaphors to change the previous stories and the previous metaphors.

Encouraging people to discover their own stories

The aim of a change workshop is very much that of encouraging people to discover their own stories and to come to realise the implications of their stories for themselves as people, for the organisation and for the work being done. There is a tendency for managers who uncover stories to do two things, neither of which is very constructive. The first one is to deny the importance of the story and not to act on what they discover, if this proves to be hindering the efforts of the organisation. The second one is to tell people the truth in a direct manner. That latter one is tempting for all those of us who have been taught that honesty is the best policy. However, in some circumstances, a too direct and honest style may not work. Too often people do not want to hear the truth, the truth being too painful for them to consider and they become very resistant. Furthermore, if the change agent is an outsider, there is a possibility that she will not be asked to work for the organisation again. If the change agent is an internal person, others will find many creative ways of making sure that she is not heard; groups have very many sanctions for deviants! The best policy is to facilitate a process which enables people to discover what is going on – so, although the change agent knows what is going on, she allows the group to unearth this and then helps them in identifying what they would like to change.

Finally, she facilitates a process where the organisation finds a more enabling and empowering story.

In the example of the training school, the head of department used an external management consultant to run a workshop to facilitate a change process. The consultant used collage and drawing to help people carry out their own organisational analysis. With the assistance of the consultant, they uncovered the victim/persecutor game they were playing. The consultant helped them to realise that the story line they had adopted was a very disempowering one. They discovered how much energy was being channelled in playing victims or persecutors, which meant that much less energy was available for the accomplishment of the task of the organisation; people felt depleted of energy.

The consultant asked them as a team to make up another collage, depicting a fitting model for the organisation. From this new story, it emerged that people were keen to be empowered. The main conclusion from the new story line was that people were determined to find out what they could personally do when faced with constraints. They were also quite resolute to place their energy in carrying out the task.

Activity 9.5

Identify the dominant stories in your work organisation.

– How can the story be changed?
– Find a new and more empowering story.

The beginning of a change process needs careful nurturing

When there has been a new start, this beginning is very fragile. The early days of a change process needs careful attention. The change agent has to take great care of the first new steps. It is very easy to revert back to old patterns and behaviours.

The external consultant had been employed by the organisation only for conducting the workshop. She knew the importance of taking care of new strategies. She ensured that someone in the organisation would work as an internal change agent and gently remind people when they lapsed into their old patterns. She also suggested that in the first 6 months, the team should meet monthly to discuss the outcomes of the workshop and using their second collage they could monitor their progress and review how they were getting on.

Helping people through the "getting worse before it gets better" phase

During a process of change, things often get worse before they get better. This is a very difficult stage for people and as we have just discussed, it is crucial to nurture the beginnings, in the same way as a new born baby requires care, otherwise he will not survive. People get very dispirited at this stage and we have to explain to them that this is a common and normal facet of transformation. Repeating old and unhelpful patterns when we have promised ourselves to change can make us feel very depressed. Therefore, it is an important function of change agents to support people during that time. What we need to do is to explain to people that behaviour patterns enacted in full consciousness are not quite the same as when we do so out of awareness. There is a different quality about it and doing things in full consciousness is half-way to total transformation. In the early days, if people do find themselves simply repeating the old patterns, all they need to do is to carry on doing these patterns **in full awareness**. A decisive step is to take personal responsibility for our behaviour. Another, more advanced phase in the change process occurs when we detect that we are about to use our old patterns and choose another more appropriate one. At a much later date, we can change the behaviour completely, making deep, fundamental changes in our value systems. Then we have undergone a total paradigm shift. However, new paradigms and new perspectives in time may become obsolete, hence the need to be forever ready to change.

No utopian promise

It is imperative for change agents not to make utopian promises when discussing change with others. We cannot say that if people do X that Y will follow. As we have seen in earlier chapters, in this world we deal constantly with uncertainty and complexity. The future is always uncertain; no-one can tell us in advance the exact outcome of a change process. There is multiple causality, not simple cause-and-effect relationships, in work organisations. The wish for utopian outcomes is understandable when faced with an uncertain world, but it is not a helpful strategy. In work organisations, fantasy is not useful. We cannot guarantee an outcome and it is very important that everyone should understand that.

Activity 9.6

Reflect on a change process you have undertaken.

– Was it difficult in the early days to maintain your new patterns?
– How did you react when you were unable to implement the change in behaviour which you had intended?

Changing what can be realistically changed – no utopia

Lord give me the courage
To change what I can change
The serenity to accept What I cannot change
And the wisdom
To know the difference.

Prayer attributed to St. Francis of Assisi

This prayer of St. Francis illustrates the crucial point that there is much in this world which we cannot change and there is so much which is not under our control. It seems that, very often, work organisations are attempting the impossible. We cannot change everything. The change agent's role is to get people to discover what it is that they cannot change and encourage them to accept that this is so. Helping people in having the serenity of acceptance is crucial. Sometimes, therefore, the change agent's role becomes one of assisting people to become aware of what they cannot change. In low- and middle-income countries, many projects appear to be attempting to change the impossible. This leads to disillusionment and demotivation as, not surprisingly, people are unable to achieve what they set out to do.

Attempting the impossible may be simply another defence strategy. It keeps people in a constant state of busy-ness and of overactivity – with little tangible outcome, as no one in this world can achieve the impossible. We are mere human beings and are not omnipotent. Achieving the possible means taking responsibility and having the courage to act in a way which leads to success. The change agent's role is to facilitate this process for others.

The organisational consultant has been asked to conduct a workshop on stress for this international NGO. The first day is spent on finding out the causes of stress in the organisation. During the discussions, it is evident that people are trying to change what cannot be changed: they want to alleviate poverty – the consultant points out that this is not under their control and encourages them to focus on a few means by which they can contribute in a very small way to the alleviation of poverty. As their stories unfold, they implicitly suggest that one of their hidden aims is that of stopping suffering in the world. The consultant encourages them to consider that this is entirely outside their control. But they have great difficulties in accepting this. It seems to the consultant that they are very distressed by the level of pain and suffering which they witness as part of their work. These emotions are not given an outlet in the organisation. The workers are also reluctant to face their own emotions. The consultant facilitates a process where they are encouraged to face their own sufferings and the pain they experience from witnessing the afflictions and misery of others. In this session, people cry openly and the consultant encourages this. She also invites them to tell their stories. At the end of the workshop, having processed these emotions, they feel energised to deal with what they can change. The consultant reads out the prayer of St. Francis to them and they proceed to carry out an exercise. First, they consider what they can realistically influence, what it is that they can change and look at whether they are doing so or not. Second, they list the things which they cannot change and which they will no longer attempt to change. The consultant helps them to look for their own hidden agendas, the implicit notions behind their work and to consider whether these are realistic or utopian.

On the importance of being realistic

Although at some level, one person working differently will have some effect on a system, an individual acting alone cannot alter a larger system. The lesson for us is to focus on the areas where we are able to do something and to save our energy for the issues which are the most relevant to us. We have to ask ourselves what we can do which will engage us in that space over which we have some control and some influence. It is important for people working in problematic large systems to become aware that there are small areas of their reality which they can influence.

Activity 9.7

– **Make a list of the things which you can change.**
– **Make a list of the other things which you cannot change.**
– **Do you have the serenity to accept what you cannot change?**
– **What are you going to do about the issues which you can change?**

Enantiodromia or the flip-over phenomenon

A phenomenon which can be useful to change agents is that of enantiodromia. This means that when a system is operating very much at an extreme, there is a tendency for it to flip-over into its opposite when a level of saturation has been reached. This phenomenon can be useful to the change agent. For example, if people are feeling very helpless, the temptation is to tell them that they should be empowered and should take personal responsibility for what they can change. Using this type of tactic is likely to make people very resistant, as we then come across as critical parents giving them a sermon about what they do wrong and telling them what to do; not the way to treat adults, and not surprisingly not liked by others who resist our efforts. A valuable strategy is to allow people to stay with their felt helplessness and to encourage them to tell their stories about their feelings of being disempowered. Without any further intervention from the change agent, after a critical point has been reached, people will automatically start to feel empowered again and hold more positive thoughts. The change agent's role is to notice when this happens – there is a change in energy level, in what people say and in their non-verbal communication. When the flip-over takes place, the change agent encourages people to consider the positives, the things they can undertake and the things they can change

The change agent has been invited to work for a week with the key workers of this NGO which provides health and disability services. It becomes obvious that there is much despair, a sense of powerlessness and of helplessness among these workers. The change agent encourages them to stay with their despair. She invites them to tell their stories. For quite a long time, people express their frustrations, their discouragement and their hopelessness. The atmosphere becomes gloomy. The workers are desolate and downcast. It seems that there is little they can achieve. Eventually however, the mood changes. This is barely perceptible at first. But the change agent notes the change and feeds back what she has observed to the group, i.e., that the level of energy has just altered. Suddenly, the whole ambience becomes very different. People start to talk about their achievements, what they have been able to do in spite of all their constraints. The words they use, the way they hold themselves, their tone of voice and their non-verbal gestures are all now very different. The workers become very energised and the whole workshop changes after this critical moment, with people becoming committed to realistic action, which they subsequently carry out.

When the solution is the problem

In first-order change, we sometimes find that the solution to an issue is in effect the problem. When people are very logical and rational in style and want very clear intentions, taking the shortest logical route to an outcome, they tend to end up with solutions which are more problematic than the original problem (Watzlawick P. et al., 1974). The mythological figure which depicts this is Oedipus who spends his life attempting in a rational manner to avoid the curse placed on him. He has clear goals to avoid his fate, but everything he does actually ensures that the original curse is carried out. He is so intent on his different actions and so determined to carry these out, that he falls into his own traps. His solutions are the problems. We can remedy this by accepting fully the complexity of the world, by being creative, by valuing the void, by embracing the flux of life and of the workplace and by allowing change to emerge rather than directing it.

In this project, there is much envy and hostility between workers. There is no sense of team work. People do not communicate well with each other. They are all hard working and do not spend time socializing. Time spent with colleagues is not seen as work. Staff meetings used to be held once a month. The project leader decides that to remedy this situation, people need to meet more often. Workers are expected to attend a regular weekly meeting and are encouraged to have a coffee break together on a daily basis. The underlying problems have not been addressed. The coffee breaks become a focus for gossip. There is interaction between people at the social level, but this is mainly superficial. Most of the time, people talk about their absent colleagues, and there are many stories about the project leader in his absence. Staff continuously complain about the project leader when he is not there but they do not give him any direct feedback. In the regular weekly meetings, the hostile interchange between people has increased. The proposed solution to remedy the problems of teamwork, i.e., meetings and coffee breaks, have become the problem, for this is where people now plan their sabotaging of the project, and where they play out the underlying unrest and conflict which has plagued this project for a long time. Things are much worse than they were before and seem to be staying that way.

In the above example, the shortest logical route to getting staff to work well together has led the project leader to coerce people into attending regular meetings and into meeting socially over coffee. There has been no attempt to face the complexity of the situation, to identify what was going wrong, the nature of the hostility and how to remedy this. Instead the solutions, i.e., more meetings and regular coffee breaks, act as a repository for the conflict and the hostility. The solutions are now the problem and the initial issue is exacerbated.

"More of the same" does not work

The above example can also be seen as an illustration of the fact that more of the same does not change a situation. There is a strong tendency for project leaders to do more of the same when something has not worked (Watzlawick P. et al., 1974).

A very important point to remember is that when something has not worked, it is crucial to stop doing more of the same thing and to try something else.

In this project, the culture is one where feelings and emotions are denied and people are not expected to have weaknesses and admit when they are not coping. Susannah likes to express her emotions. In her work as a trainer and facilitator, she cannot help but work with emotions. She often feels drained at the end of sessions and would like to be able to share how she feels with her colleagues. Sometimes there are so many workshops, that she is totally overwhelmed. She would like more support from her colleagues; at times all she needs is simply someone to listen to her. She has brought up the topic at several staff meetings. She has also discussed this issue with her immediate manager. Although people acknowledge that a regular support group would be useful, her various attempts have not led to any action. She keeps bringing up the issue of support for staff but no one seems to take what she says seriously. At the last planning meeting, she again placed this issue on the agenda. When the time came to discuss support for staff, there was an uneasy silence and no one spoke. Susannah felt very discouraged. When she joined this organisation, she quickly learned that to be considered a competent worker in this project, she should not admit to not coping and must hide her real feelings and emotions. This is a culture which does not allow emotions in the workplace. Recently, she has been going through a difficult time. Her workshops are highly successful. But as she is so sensitive and gives so much of herself, she has been ill, her defences are low and she is feeling stressed and overwhelmed. However, she has now realised that she was simply "doing more of the same". She has decided to try something very different. At the last staff meeting, she talked about the difficulties she was experiencing and revealed how upset she was after a specific incident. Her colleagues are very surprised by what she says. Susannah is a strong, competent worker. They have never seen her as this vulnerable human being, easily hurt by comments. She is the one they go to see when they need help. As a result, it is noticeable that people in the organisation have started to talk more freely about their emotions. A few people have also revealed some of their own difficulties. There has been a friendlier atmosphere in the project, and more reaching out towards other people in staff meetings. Occasionally, there have even been some offers of help. Susannah has also received these offers.

When we work as change agents, we have to find out what people are doing to remedy their predicaments, and ask how effective are their strategies. If they are simply repeating more of the same with no result, they need to be encouraged to try something else.

The paradox of change

We meet paradox once again as change often occurs when we least expect it, with an alteration taking place when we have stopped trying. If we try too hard, things do not alter. And sometimes, it is when we give up trying to change, that something actually happens. The change agent therefore stimulates change and lets go of the need to change, appreciating the mystery involved and allowing things to happen and allowing life to take its course.

Hassana came to this project after completing a management course where the emphasis was on treating people with dignity and respect. She was quite upset to find that her colleagues did not share her values. They viewed themselves as superior to the local people. Hassana tried many times to change their attitudes but with no success. She has decided to work differently from her colleagues in a way which respects the dignity of other human beings. She is no longer attempting to change her colleagues. She now notices that they are also becoming more respectful of the local community. At the last project meeting, they talked about ways to involve the community in the project and someone pointed out that there were many talents among the local people which the project should recognise.

Doing while "not doing": working as a "rainmaker"

As we saw in the last chapter, small interventions lead to important outcomes. For the change agent, this means doing as little as possible, going where people are, following their energy, following the weird ways of work organisations and often simply waiting for things to happen. This is yet another paradox: intervention and no intervention. Sometimes this is called working as a rainmaker or working with presence. Rainmakers in traditional societies often did not do very much. They arrived and the rains came. Just being there is an intervention. Simply listening and feeding back to people what we observe are very powerful interventions.

Not "why" questions, but "what" and "how"

For the change agent in work organisations, "why" questions are not very interesting. As we have discussed earlier, there is inevitably multi-causality in work settings. In the complex world of organisations, there rarely are simple causes and effects. In addition, it is not true that we have to understand causality to be able to effect change. But "what" and "how" questions are very important to the change agent. What are people doing, what are the patterns, how are the patterns maintained, what can be changed, how can these be changed? This type of questioning is valuable to the change agent as it encourages movement into the future and opens the door to new possibilities.

The rationality of "irrational" behaviour

When we function as change agents we often observe what to us appears to be irrational behaviour in work organisations. We have to remember that what may appear illogical to us may be perfectly rational from the point of view of those who adopt this behaviour. There are multiple perspectives and the viewpoints of others are as valid as ours. What may be dysfunctional can also serve a purpose and, unless we understand the function of these patterns, we cannot help people and the organisation to change. Pathologizing and labelling others are not helpful when we are encouraging them to change.

In this hospital, there is much stress and tension. Resources are very inadequate; there are no effective managerial and administrative systems. The doctors are becoming very distressed. They often do not have the drugs necessary for patients. They do know that many people have died because of the inadequacies of the hospital or because of the lack of resources available to them. Those who have been here a long time are quite desensitised to the situation. They are remote from patients, treat them as objects and appear callous in their dealings with patients.

The above example illustrates how unreasonable behaviour – treating patients as objects – serves a function and is "logical". These doctors have been taught to save lives and are unable to do so because of inefficiencies and lack of resources. In such a situation, they are inevitably distressed. A change agent, working in that context, would need to become aware that the poor relationship of doctors to patients is a defence strategy which protects these doctors from experiencing too much distress and too much pain, in the light of not being able to carry out what they have been trained for.

In this multi-disciplinary project, the coordinators from the different specialities are always confronting each other and arguing in a non-constructive manner. Meetings are the focus of these unpleasant confrontations. The rest of the staff remain passive and watch the same people arguing. The atmosphere has become so unpleasant that they have called in an external consultant. He quickly becomes aware that the coordinators seem to be enjoying these conflicting situations, they seem to thrive on the high levels of energy generated – it appears to be some sort of addictive behaviour. But they are not the only ones gaining thrills from this situation; it is obvious that the staff members looking on are also thoroughly enjoying the show. In working with this group of people, the consultant makes them aware of what is going on. They agree that there is not much excitement in the present stage of the project and that they are starting to be bored with the task at hand. The consultant discusses with them alternative ways of finding interest, stimulation and high energy so that they do not seek this through endless disputes.

The important consideration for the change agent is to focus on what is happening in the here and now which is allowing an issue to persist and what it is that can be done to generate a change to a more useful pattern.

"Both… and…" revisited

In the world of work, as we have seen in the earlier chapters, answers are rarely of the "either… or…" variety. Yet this is what people have a tendency to do. If there is something which we do not favour, we tend to settle for an "either… or…" position; therefore if we do not like X, we avoid X or prevent X from happening. What we often fail to do is to look for totally different solutions outside the frame of either "X" or "not X". For second-level change, it is important to abstain from dichotomies and to find an answer from the paradox which we meet as discussed in the earlier chapter on decision-making.

Reframing revisited

As we saw earlier, we can encourage people to re-frame a situation, to give a different meaning to what is happening, to carry out a figure/ground reversal. We see the same thing but with new eyes. We can inspire people to look at any situation in a creative manner. The act of giving another name to a situation is a very potent one. Conflict in a work setting can be re-named as opportunity for creative ideas. We can reframe the concept itself: conflict as positive and not negative. We can reframe the emotional context, fear can become excitement, anger can become energy for action. We can reframe the perspective; for example, we can see a situation in a community project from the perspective of the village leaders, from the perspective of the local children and of the women in that community instead of the perspective of the professionals involved in the project.

Mohamed has recently attended a workshop aimed at providing project leaders with interpersonal skills. He is now back at work where there is much conflict and where some people are rather "difficult". He used to be very unhappy in this work setting, as he personally prefers a more supportive, less conflictual setting. However, he has to work for this organisation as there are not many opportunities for paid work in this part of the country. In reframing the situation, he now sees dealing with his difficult colleagues as an opportunity to practice his skills. His emotional reframing includes turning his anxiety into the energy which he requires to deal with a challenging situation. This reframing means that he is now much happier in working for this project.

Working with so-called "resistance"

When we encourage people to change, they may not be willing or ready to follow us. This phenomenon is what change agents usually call "resistance". Moreover, the tendency is to counteract "resistance" which usually leads to even more opposition. What we need to confront as change agents is the fact that we see people as resisting when they do not wish to do as we think they should. This is an arrogant and superior ("I'm O.K. – You're not O.K." position) and as change agents we need to recognise what we are doing. A first step is to accept and acknowledge people's right to be very different from us without the need to change them. If we encounter "resistance", it often means that people may not be ready/willing to change and we need to accept that. It may also mean that we have used the wrong intervention, or that we have missed out on some important aspect of our communication, or that maybe we are not listening carefully and that we need to work on our relationship with other people. It is much wiser to simply follow people and to allow them to take us where they want. We need to wait until perhaps they are ready to address the issues which we would like them to consider while engaging in constructive conversations with them and focusing on our relationship with them. Additionally, we also accept that what we are proposing may not be for them and we respect and support their wishes not to change.

On the importance of questions

Often in organisations, solutions are applied as a result of asking the wrong questions. In complex situations, it is easy to do so. The obvious questions may not be the ones to ask. Issues often hide much deeper ones and we need to ensure that we are asking the right questions. To avoid falling into the trap of following the wrong lead, we have to define the problem very clearly in very specific and concrete terms. It is also important to look very closely at the solutions which have already been tried. This is an important step as it tells us which interventions we must not use if we do not want to keep repeating the "more of the same" pattern. Finally, we clearly define the desired practical outcome of change. These steps help us in clarifying whether or not we are asking the correct questions.

Activity 9.8

Consider a problem or a challenge which you face at work.

– **Are you looking for easy solutions?**
– **Are you spending enough time considering the important questions to ask?**
– **Use "what" and "how" questions to enable you to see the issue more clearly.**

However, in a complex and uncertain world, we also need to accept that there are often no answers. Raising the questions and reflecting on those without searching for solutions may be paradoxically the best "solution".

Introducing confusion to bring about change

This point has been addressed implicitly in the early section of this chapter. Here, I simply want to point out that introducing confusion is an important means of facilitating deep change. Traditional societies used confusion as a means of initiating people into new roles (second-order change) during periods of transition. Confusion was introduced through a variety of means: experiencing hunger, having to find one's way back home from an unknown place, sleeping during the day and being active at night. In the private sector, organisations occasionally use some of these very explicit examples of confusion. A large organisation in Europe, during a major change process, held meetings in the middle of the night while people rested during the day. We do not have to use extreme cases to introduce confusion so that change may occur. This is what we are doing when we "disturb the field". By changing the focus, we often disturb the field.

Importance of unplanned and trivial incidents

Often profound change can occur from totally unplanned or very trivial incidents. This is a humbling phenomenon for the change agent and sometimes leaving the course of events to providence may lead to second-order change in an unplanned manner. The lesson for change agents is that when we have succeeded in achieving a change process, we have to be very grateful about the positive outcome and remain very humble about "our" achievements. The reverse is that when we do not succeed, it is important not to be upset and distraught, remembering the mystery of the process of working and living.

Self-care of the change agent

Change agents work at the chaotic edge. An important role is that of helping others cope with the void, of facilitating the acceptance that often, in life and in work, things get worse before they get better. They also assist others in dealing with fear, anxiety, apprehension, scepticism and despair. This is no easy task. Therefore, change agents themselves have to be in a satisfactory state of well-being. Their self-care is extremely important. Their aim is to generate eustress for themselves while avoiding distress. As ordinary mortals, change agents will also experience their own doubts and difficulties. Furthermore, when we deal with change, it is important that we ourselves have some elements of stability in our own lives. The concept of stability zones is a useful one in ensuring that we do get the support which we require to do this type of work. Stability zones are parts of our lives: people and things which are always there for us when we need to pause, to reconnect and to be grounded. These can be people or organisations: partners, friends, supervisors, managers, teachers, a club, a religious or other group who are available to us to nurture and sustain us when this is what we require. They can be places we go to, for example, a special chair in a bedroom, a quiet place in the house, a favourite walk, a garden, etc., where we can retire and feel safe. They can be objects and things which give us pleasure and peace. They can also be ideas, philosophies, values and spiritual beliefs which we hold and which guide us and give us sustenance. We need at least one stability zone in our lives, but it is preferable to have a number of those, so that if one is not available for any reason, we can fall back on others.

Activity 9.9

Think through the stability zones in your life.

– How good are they?
– Will they save and support you when you require that help?
– Do you need to add to your list of stability zones?

The magician and the scientist

The change agent has been described as working both as a scientist – hence the principles outlined in this book – and at the same time as working as a magician, i.e., in a completely mysterious way. In the same way, the change agent uses both left and right brain hemispheres, moving from the two different ways of dealing with the world whenever this is appropriate. Change agents therefore work as traditional healers, as magicians, as shamans and as rainmakers (Mindell A., 1995), although they study and research the principles of a change process in a scientific way. The magical part is unfortunately something which cannot be gained from a book – we cultivate this part by developing ourselves, by movement from the inner self to the outer and by trusting our own intuition and our creativity. These skills are crucial if we want to be effective managers and effective change agents. Hence, the need for us to embark on our personal journeys for our own development and to discover our talents and how to use these talents in our workplace, and how through our work we can contribute to the well-being of the universe.

Activity 9.10

Possible workshops to consider how a project could improve:

(a) Hold a "where are we going" day – use both left and right brain material.
   – Usually on these occasions, we find that needs and resources do not match; if this is so, feed back this finding to people, encourage them to face that this is the way things are and get people to concentrate on what they can do.

(b) Focus on the following questions to form the basis of a workshop:
   – What has happened before in the organisation?
   – What have people tried which worked?
   – What have people tried which failed?
   – How can it be made to work, what are the learning points from these so-called failures?
   – How can the organisation move forward?

(c) Using collage, drawings, playdough, metaphors and stories explore the following:
   – Where are we?
   – What are the ways forward?
   – Analyse the stories.
   – Find better stories.

(d) Find ways to gather information anonymously to find out, what people would like to say but do not dare say. Get the secrets and the myths out in the open.

(e) Use "If...then..." exercises to find out what people in the organisation believe.

(f) Encourage people to consider their personal goals,
   then ask them to consider the goals of the organisation,
   finally, explore how the two can be reconciled and how they can best serve the wider society and by extension the universe.

WITH ALL THE ABOVE, END BY LOOKING AT THE CHOICES WHICH PEOPLE HAVE. SUPPORT THEM IN NOT CHANGING WHEN THINGS CANNOT BE CHANGED AND HELP THEM WITH REALISTIC POSSIBLE CHANGES.

Therefore as change agents, we acknowledge the mystery in deep transformation. We appreciate the conundrum of a complex world with its unknown and unknowable future. We accept that we are not in control. But at the same time we discover what it is that we can influence. We engage in meaningful conversations with others around us, focusing on developing deep relationships and, through our spontaneous self-organisation, we become the co-creators of the future for ourselves and for the wider society. As we come to the end of this book, we remember our interconnectedness in this world and the importance of continuously unlearning and changing.

Bon voyage!

Reference and further reading

Mindell A. (1995) *METASKILLS – the spiritual art of therapy*, New falcon Publications, Tempe, Arizona, USA.

Watzlawick P., Weakland J. and Fisch R. (1974) *Changes, principles of problem formation and problem resolution*, Norton, New York.

Rumi (l991) *One-handed Basked Weaving – Poems on the Theme of Work*, Versions by Coleman Barks, Maypop, Athens, Georgia.